Discovering
GOD'S
Love

More Books in the Series:

Discovering God's Sufficiency
Going beyond ourselves and experiencing the supernatural
Pastoral Health Care — Part One

Discovering God's Counsel
Applying his spiritual solution to meet difficult trials
Pastoral Health Care — Part Three

Discovering God's Kingdom
Finding a way to understand ourselves in a complex world
Pastoral Health Care – Part Four

Discovering God's Heart
Feeling God's heart pulse is our daily challenge
Pastoral Health Care — Part Five

"I have ALS which means that my life is being taken away from me. Don't ask me how I am doing. Every day brings new challenges but I am learning to live each moment with God's presence. I am comforted knowing that the Holy Spirit is traveling each step with me. I ask for his filling every day and even every hour. I am assured of my future with Jesus. As I meditate on his Word, he provides me with his perspective on life — death and all the stuff in between. I will reach my destiny with my team supporters."

— *Cindy Smith*

"I am 100 years old and have all the special physical needs that people my age experience. The spiritual Biblical mediation method works for me. It has strengthened my faith. As I recite the promises, they become a part of my thinking process. My fellowship with God provides natural growth for me both internally and externally. I am thankful that I live with His presence."

— *William Mulder*

"I have grown up with seizures. I know what it is like to lose consciousness. I know my illness is a brain disorder that requires prescribed medicines regularly. Adjusting to the various dosages is a pain. I hate the side effects that I live with. I am enabled through the guidance of the Bible. It keeps reminding me of 'His' nearness. I am thankful for the support I have. I miss my former life and its activities. My prayer is always "keep me close to you, God, and my family!" Discovering God's Sufficiency has challenged me to be close to Jesus Christ."

— *George Odiorne*

"My Life has always looked a little different. I was born with spina bifida and fluid on my brain. I have to live with many side effects like sore back, loss of balance, terrible headaches and short term memory. I have been able to manage every day remembering that God has a purpose for my life. I have been blessed with a family that I need to be here for. Every day brings new challenges that have turned my spirit toward Scripture. To my amazement, God has promised to help me. I can't count the times that I have felt His presence. I know that God has a plan for me and he will accomplish it according to his will."

— *Judy Sharp*

"I have had MS for several years. At the present time, I have been experiencing intense nerve pain. My relationship with Christ has helped me make the adjustments that are needed to survive. I am comforted to know that I will not be stretched beyond my ability to bear. I have confidence that God's will will be accomplished in my life. I have my destiny in heaven where I will experience perfection. I know abiding in Christ is the key."

— *Chuck Boomgard*

"I live with Multiple Sclerosis which is a neurological disease that affects every part of my body. I never know from one day to the next how my body is going to be. I have more MS days than functional days. While losing my worldly independence, I have gained a powerful relationship with my God by choosing to depend upon him. My trust in God empowers me to face every day with joy."

— *Susan Clark Denny*

John's books give us hope and light. He reminds us that through Jesus we are never alone. I have certainly needed that reminder in my life and in my practice. In holding a patient's hand, and helping them through a condition or disease, reminding them that they are never alone has become the greatest gift of health care.

— Linda M. Kunce, D.C.

As a Christian who made a commitment to follow Christ as a teen, I have had my share of struggles. In using the book, "Discovering God's Love" it was good to read that Jesus knows what its like to live in a human body. I have received Jesus and His forgiveness, but as the book suggests, I also have power from the Holy Spirit. I should lean on Jesus. Perhaps I can be more secure in meeting the challenges of life. His book encouraged me to gain courage through prayer. The author's honesty is very special to read in this book as he reflects on his own life and struggles. I like his explanation that "the soul is where the emotions are and the mind is where the thinking takes place."

It was good for me to read that God works through weakness, and learn that the author found God with him in the middle of his struggles. My interest was peaked by the questions in Chapter 10. The answers in the book really show why we should follow Jesus. As to love, the book states that God's love is freely given and we show love by touch, words, time and excitement. Quoting Pastor Gillette, I appreciated that he sees life involved in many things, including love. God sees us as His glorious inheritance. Wonderful. Praise God!

—Arvid W. Vandyke, Ed.D.

True, illustrative, practical stories are like windows that unlock Bible truths and promises.

Along with masterfully orchestrated short stories should come the truth that God's Word and love has been experienced by His servants as they partner with Him in the work of rebuilding the Kingdom.

Dr. Gillette has done just that in this second book of four relating to life's essential and persistent questions posed to ministers. A gifted teacher, Dr. Gillette lives an ordinary life abiding in Christ and being an obedient servant of the Lord. As he sees God working in his life, and in the lives of those to whom he ministers, his faith is refreshed and he is encouraged to press on through life's uncertainties.

One day, I was "pressing" John for more stories of how he has experienced or seen God's love demonstrated in his own life, and in the lives of his congregants and students. He said to me, "Dr. Mulonge, in pastoring and teaching there are many days, some filled with joy and others marked with pain, that's just life." Thank God for the "all the days" that teach the mighty works, the power and matchless love of God.

Only a lifetime dedicated to nurturing, ministering, teaching, and keen insight through the power of the Holy Spirit, can produce such poignant stories that teach and challenge. Dr. Gillette has done exactly this once again.

—*Mulonge M. Kalumbula, Ph.D.*

I believe in God's sovereignty and compassion. I am learning to let go of self and to hold onto someone that can do whatever he pleases. Sometimes life is cruel, sometimes it is full of suffering, physically and psychological. A spiritual solution to meet difficult trials has become my goal. God's word carries with it no uncertainties. I want it to saturate my mind and heart.

The *Pastoral Health Care* series was created through unexpected heart disease (open heart surgery), cancer (medication and surgery), a stroke and major head injury after a car accident that also resulted in the death of my wife. I am writing this because it is helping me to develop an adequate level to supernatural, psychological and physiological adjustments. It may help you as well. It has brought me security.

—*John F. Gillette, D.Min.*

Discovering GOD'S *Love*

Confirming God's Love through the evidence of historical facts

JOHN F. GILLETTE
WITH JOY E. GILLETTE
Author of Discovering God's Favor

Chapbook Press

Schuler Books
2660 28th Street SE
Grand Rapids MI 49512

www.schulerbooks.com/chapbook-press

Discovering God's Love: Confirming God's love through the evidence of historical facts

Copyright ©2016 — John F. Gillette. All rights reserved. Published 2016. Printed at Schuler Books, Chapbook Press, Grand Rapids, Michigan, in the United States of America.

First Edition 2016

Excerpts taken from Discovering God's Presence: A Pastoral Health Care Devotional, © 2015 by Dr. John F. Gillette, D.Min.

Distribution contact:at jjgillette@comcast.net.

ISBN 13: 9781943359523

Library of Congress Control Number: 2016960220

Cover photo: Greg Rakozy/Unsplash
Cover Design: Frank Gutbrod Graphic Design

Printed in the United States of America

The Pastoral Health Care Discovery Series was produced to help during difficult trials in life. It was developed through five volumes.

Adjustments are shared through God's sufficiency. It provides a basic spiritual solution strategy. We have to affirm, accept and adjust to God's plan of action. His superiority, sovereignty and sufficiency will bring victory.

Empowerment is given through God's love. The receiving of his Son Jesus Christ provides power. Historical facts declare the truth.

Enablement is given through God's counsel. Instruction, illumination and application provides the growing process in grace.

Encouragement is given through the awareness of God's kingdom. Learning to accept God's perspective is necessary. The Holy Spirit will travel with us in the present and the future.

Contentment is given through God's heart. The meditation model is the method to follow.

It is with great affection that I dedicate this book series to my wife, Joy, who radiates God's grace. We wrote this Pastoral Health Care Series together.

Applying God's spiritual solutions to meet us in difficult trials has become even more practical in my life with the recent death of my dear wife, Joy. This book has been reproduced in her memory. While the content is the same, my dedication has become more personal than ever before. The separation is painful but as I gather my suffering and feelings of incompleteness, I will succeed with God's peace and presence. The guidelines of this book have brought blessing to our life together. We have pursued them with great persistence. I am assured that she is in God's presence, rejoicing and at peace. I will be with her to experience God's eternal presence someday as well.

". . . blessed are they who put their trust in Him."
Psalm 2:12

*This book is lovingly dedicated to my daughter,
Amy Joy Gillette
who has discovered God's love and confirms
it in her life every day.*

Table of Contents

Introduction 01

Chapter 1
Jesus Christ Humanity
What is the Basis for Authority in the Gospel of Luke? 04

Chapter 2
What Knowledge is Necessary to Accept the Gospel? 08

Chapter 3
Are There Any Witnesses for the Gospel? 13

Chapter 4
What Victory Does the Gospel Provide? 25

Chapter 5
Who Is the Primary Focus of the Gospel? 34

Chapter 6
What Is the Basis of Courage Found in The Gospel? 37

Chapter 7
What Part Does the Heart Have in the Gospel? 41

Chapter 8
How Does Jesus Show His Compassion in the Gospel? 48

Chapter 9
Jesus Christ Deity
Who is Jesus Christ? 54

Chapter 10
Why Follow Jesus Christ? 57

Chapter 11
What Should Be Included in Worshipping Jesus Christ? 65

Chapter 12
What Does It Mean to be Selected by God? 69

Chapter 13
What Part Does Conflict Play in Jesus Christ's Ministry? 73

Chapter 14
What Does the Abundant Life Refer To? 82

Chapter 15
How Does Feeling Good About Jesus Christ Work? 86

Chapter 16
What Is Involved in Praising Jesus Christ? 94

Chapter 17
What is a Permanent Badge of Discipleship? 101

Chapter 18
Where Can I Find Comfort in These Days? 106

Chapter 19
What Does Remaining in Jesus Christ mean? *112*

Chapter 20
How Does Remaining in Jesus Christ Involve Prayer? *117*

Chapter 21
What Part Does Remaining in Jesus Christ Have to Do with Intercession? *123*

Chapter 22
How Often Do We Deny Jesus Christ? *128*

Chapter 23
Why Did Jesus Christ Die? *134*

Chapter 24
What is Supernatural About Jesus Christ's Death? *137*

Chapter 25
What Motivates Active Faith in Jesus Christ's Death and Resurrection? *140*

Sources *143*

Acknowledgements *146*

Introduction

Discovering God's Love provides the spiritual solution source of power. Jesus Christ Is the perfect man. In the Gospel of Luke, his ministry is described with kindness, tenderness and agony. He understands our needs. He can sympathize with us in a personal way. He also has power to enable us in our trials. The Gospel of John proves that Jesus is God incarnate in human flesh. He knows what it is like to live in the human body and, at the same time, be divine.

Things do not just happen. Everything that occurs does so under the hand of the sovereign God. There is no chance happening, no luck, no mistakes and both good and bad fall under his control. We can live with authority because he is in charge. God is unique and he is one of a kind. We cannot compare him to anyone else. Nothing else in the universe is like him. We have to understand God on his terms. He will provide understanding and he is incomprehensible. Yet through his characteristics, he can be known. Each attribute will provide us with power. Just think of it, "people who know their God will display strength and take action" (Daniel 11:32).

It starts with activating these words "he that believeth on me" (John 7:38). We have to receive the truth of Jesus Christs' death and resurrection for the forgiveness of sin in our hearts. Then "from within him shall flow rivers of living water." The reception of the Holy Spirit through belief opens the door to his power (John 1:12). God will never give divine power in order that we may do our will. Divine power is always found in line with divine purpose. The secret of power use is being in agreement with his will. The apostles have said that God gives the Holy Spirit to them that obey (Acts 5:32). Obedience creates selflessness and selflessness requires reliance. God never gives power to store up for use. God is sovereign and it lies with him to determine the amount, the extent and the character of filling. We are sufficient in him because the gospels declare it.

It seems like I have visited many specialists over the past few of years. I have added one more specialist to my list. This doctor was spoken of as a "beloved physician." He was a friend and useful companion of Paul's (Acts 1:1; Colossians 4:4c). He was a reliable historian, a scholar and a sympathetic doctor (Luke 1:1-3; Acts 1:1-3). He had superior qualifications as a co-worker with Paul (servant, missionary, scholar) with many personal eyewitness acquaintances and the Holy Spirit's inspiration. Dr. Luke's mission was to proclaim Christs' humanity.

I have learned to trust this human, yet divine Jesus. He is the spiritual source of power and provides confidence and love for daily living.

Jesus Christ Humanity

What is the Basis for Authority in the Gospel of Luke?

As a trained physician, Luke gave detailed accounts of the birth of two important babies. He emphasized Christ's sympathy for hurting people. He would write with the mind of a careful historian and with the heart of a loving physician. He wrote an accurate and orderly narrative of the life, ministry and message of Jesus Christ. He carefully researched his material, interviewed eyewitnesses and listened to those who had ministered the Word.

The acceptance of Biblical authority is necessary. After listening to the specialists in regard to my diseases, I turned to Dr. Luke's emphasis on Biblical authority. I have been challenged in my life and have been given confidence. The biography of Christ found in the book of Luke provides the knowledge that the "Son of Man" (Jesus) has experienced my grief and sorrow and he is able to meet those needs. The genius of the Scripture has produced God's Word for me. "Most surely believed" — Luke pens a complete history of the events surrounding the beginning, growth and development of Christianity. It is possible that some of Luke's sources were word-of-mouth reports. The truth of the Gospel is authoritative, logical and factual.

"Eyewitnesses and ministers of the Word" — Luke's information came from eyewitnesses who had seen the very beginning of the Gospel account. He must have met some of the twelve original disciples. Hundreds if not thousands of people who had personally heard Jesus teach would become a witness to the story of Jesus. I would have liked to hear those testimonies in a court of law. "Having had perfect understanding" — these words refer to the divine revelation he received from the Holy Spirit (2 Timothy 3:16,

2 Peter 1:19-21). His investigation, research and interviews would become the evidence for me to trust the authority of the Bible. As I have looked at the qualifications and abilities of my doctors, I have used the same process to accept Dr. Luke's information.

He shares the supernatural testimony of four ordinary people. Zacharias (Jehovah has remembered) and Elisabeth (God is my oath) were a godly couple who both belonged to the priestly line. They lived faithful lives in obedience to the Word of God. Constant prayer brought into their home a baby that would herald the coming King. Read their story. Their faith was blessed and their unbelief was judged. God kept his promise "there is nothing too hard for the Lord" (Jeremiah 32:17). Their baby's name was John (Jehovah is gracious). My name is John. I can certainly testify of God's graciousness in my life (Discovering God's Favor).

Joseph and Mary have been brought to my attention who were the earthly parents of Jesus (Jehovah is salvation). Jesus' deity and humanity is affirmed. As Mary's son, he would be human. The words, a son of the highest (v.32), refer to the fact that he is the Son of God (v.35). He would be the son of God (v.35). "For unto us a child is born (humanity), unto us a son is given (deity)" (Isaiah 9:6). Miracles, angels, unexpected circumstances, physical impossibilities and supernatural involvement play in the giving of confidence and assurance that the Bible is true. This is confirmation that I can rest firmly upon the historical facts.

What Knowledge is Necessary to Accept the Gospel?

Dr. Luke gives me a glimpse into the early years of the Lord Jesus. Jesus comes to live among sinners, love them, help them and die for them. His life would be the fulfillment of divine prophecy. Mary, his mother, said "Be it unto me according to thy Word" (1:38). Her life would be a part of this prophecy. God promised that the Savior would be a human, not an angel (Genesis 3:15; Hebrews 2:16), a Jew and not a Gentile (Genesis 12:1-3; Numbers 24:17). He would be from the tribe of Judah (Genesis 49:10) and the family of David (2 Samuel 7:1-17), born of a virgin (Isaiah 7:14) in Bethlehem, the city of David (Micah 5:2).

I am writing this in a difficult time of history. Everything seems to be out of control. Watch any TV analysis, listen to the radio, read the newspaper and magazines or discuss the issues with someone. The events of history are hopeless but if God's Word controls my life, then the events of history only help me to fulfill the will of God (Jeremiah 1:12). King Herod (1:5) was ruthless and cunning. He loved grand building projects. Some of the ruins can be seen today in Israel. "In those days, there went out a decree from Caesar Augustus" (2:1). He was declared by the Roman Senate the first emperor. He was honored with the title "Augustus," a term signifying religious veneration. He was the supreme military power. He died at the age of seventy-six (A.D.14). Jesus' lifetime on earth was a difficult time as well — worse than mine even with all the conflicts in the world today. King Herod was masterful and merciless and is remembered for his massacre of the innocent, the murder of several of his sons and for his own appalling death. Immorality, political unrest, world power and self-exultation to deity was apparent everywhere.

Jesus was born to poor earthly parents. They traveled from Nazareth to Bethlehem about seventy miles through mountainous terrain. It must have been a grueling journey for a mother about to deliver a baby. After delivery, Jesus was wrapped in long bands of cloth to give the limbs strength and protection. It was a sign of parental care. He was placed in a manger which was a feeding trough for animals. The first announcement of Jesus' birth was given by an angel to some anonymous shepherds. Shepherds were outcasts in Israel. In Jesus' birth, he calls the poor and the lowly (I Corinthians 1:26-29; Luke 1:51-53). God selected hardworking men to be the first witness that his Son had come into the world. One of the key themes of the Christmas story is found in the words "fear not" (1:13,30,74; Matthew 1:20). Fear is a normal response. Have I ever been confronted by a divine visitation or a mighty work of God? All the miraculous events associated with Jesus' coming would cause a heart to marvel. With my salvation in Jesus Christ, I have experienced a mighty work of God. Faith and obedience are central thoughts surrounding Jesus' birth. This miracle baby became a child.

"What think ye of Christ" (Matthew 22:42; I John 4:1-3) is the most important question anybody can answer.

Three important testimonials are shared in his childhood. The presentation to the Lord (2:20-24), Simeon (2:25-35) and Anna (2:36-38). Jesus came to fulfill the law (Matthew 5:17,18). Jesus' parents obeyed the law by having Jesus circumcised when he was eight days old. This was the sign and seal of the covenant that God made with Abraham. It symbolized the work the Savior did on the cross in dealing with my sin nature (Colossians 2:10,11; Philippians 3:1-3; Galatians 6:15). He has set me free from bondage.

Simeon looked for the Messiah (Malachi 3:16). He saw Jesus in the temple. He lifted Jesus into his arms and uttered a special prophecy. He spoke of Christ as a light for the Gentiles and the glory of Israel. He truly would become my substitute for sin on the cross. Old Testament prophecy was fulfilled. The redeemer has come. I am thankful that I have obtained this salvation in my childhood and have been able to grow up in Jesus.

The third testimony is Anna who was a prophetess. This refers to a woman who spoke God's Word. She lived on the temple grounds. Her name means grace and she was a godly woman. She served God by worship through fasting and prayer. She would share the good news.

In his youth, he would develop physically, mentally, socially and spiritually. The hidden years in Nazareth were years of submission to the Father (Philippians 2:1-11). He worked in the carpenter's shop and ran the business after Joseph died. At twelve, he spent time in the temple in the midst of teachers. The teachers were amazed at both his questions and his answers. Jesus was moved by a divine compulsion to the Father's will.

Jesus has been my example during my childhood. He grew in a balanced way. His priority was to do God's will. He knew how to listen and to ask the right questions. He would have to work and obey his parents. Eighteen years later, when he emerged from Nazareth, God the Father was able to say, "thou art my beloved son; in thee I am well pleased" (Luke 3:22).

Are There Any Witnesses for the Gospel?

John the Baptist's birth and life was miraculous. His parents were beyond years to bear a son. He was the forerunner of Christ. He stands with one hand in the Old Testament and the other hand in the New Testament. He makes the transition from law and grace. He is the foreclosure of the old and the forerunner of the new. His name means 'God is gracious.' He practiced self-denial and emerges with spiritual strength. Here are some remarkable statements about his life. "Elisabeth was filled with the Holy Ghost" (Luke 1:41). She spoke with prophetic words and praise to Almighty God. She was the first woman to confess Jesus in the flesh. She is the mother of John. "And they were righteous before God" (1:6). Zachariah and Elisabeth, the parents of John, were both godly in their lives. As a matter of fact, his father had the unique opportunity of offering incense before the Holy of Holies in the temple as a priest. "The Word of God came unto John" (3:2). In the solitude of the desert, he heard the voice of God. He was familiar with the Old Testament and was in touch with God. He would become a prophet. "He preached the baptism of repentance for the remission of sins" (3:3). His message was a cleansing of the heart and a preparedness to receive the Messiah. His ministry was to prepare the way for the Messiah's appearance. It demanded a change in one's life (3:8). "I baptize you with water but one mightier than I cometh and shall baptize you with the Holy Ghost" (3:16).

On the day of Pentecost, the Holy Spirit would take up permanent residence in the bodies of the believing disciples. Based on my belief in Christ's death and resurrection through the process of faith, he dwells in me. A celebrated life in Christ is possible through the Holy Spirit's indwelling. "Thou art my beloved Son" (3:22).

The Holy Spirit speaks to the people words in the shape of a dove at Jesus' baptism. This marks the beginning of Christ's public ministry. The grace of Jesus Christ, the love of God and the communion of the Holy Ghost — all the persons of the Godhead are mentioned together to introduce Jesus Christ.

John's life gives me an example to follow. If I follow it, boldness will characterize my life in Jesus. This boldness is triggered by the Holy Spirit and is absolutely necessary. I am challenged to accept the example. His lifestyle of self-denial is a priority to follow. This is seen in his simple dress, food and environment. I think it was primarily seen in his message. This message was repentance for sin and a changed lifestyle. It was stern and demanding. Making a complete turnaround in behavior is necessary.

Self-denial and selflessness go hand in hand to produce boldness. This boldness is based upon my major focus on Jesus Christ. It is not me and what I think but rather what God thinks. Am I a devoted servant? Do I have the compassion to love the poorest of the poor? Is my conscience directed by my belief system which has its foundation in Jesus Christ? Have I been driven to share my prosperity (middle class) with anyone that needs it even if it requires doing without? Caring for others and the less fortunate should always be a character trait to desire. A deep desire to live up to the moral examples of the Scriptures and sensitivity to God's purpose has been the goal. Authentic self-denial will provide personal joy and peace. I have to learn to put my hand in God's hand and walk all the way with him. The heart has to hear from God and this is accomplished through listening to his Word. Read the Word, meditate on the Word, study the Word, apply the Word and share the Word through a personal Christ-like lifestyle. Self-denial might cause some loneliness and anxiety. It may bring a loss of some friends or cause criticism. It will also bring contentment and the illumination by the Holy Spirit. A deep sense of accomplishment can be achieved through self-denial. As I learn to sacrifice, I will glorify my creator.

Another characteristic that will produce boldness is humility. John said, "There cometh one mightier than I after me, the latchet of whose shoes I am not worthy to stoop down and unloose" (Mark 1:7). In essence, John is saying that he cannot affect the inner person. The one whom John introduces will transform the soul by the washing of regeneration and renewing of the Holy Ghost. He is only the forerunner. He is the prophet that connects the Old Testament and New Testament. He is a servant of the king to come and the eternal kingdom. His message is only a preparation step. Jesus is the Savior of the world. A man of humility is one that can weep because he knows what is in the future. He knows the destiny of the human soul. He would ask the question, "how can I serve and reach more people?" I will do anything that is in God's will to make this possible. When humility is practiced, it will bring satisfaction. It will want glory and honor for others and not self. Jealousy, bickering and suspicion are the opposite to humility. Discipline, self-reliance, courage and confidence are all examples of humility. Humility is displayed with hard work, trust, ambition and accomplishment. To do one's best, to keep the brain and conscience clear, never to be swayed by unworthy motives or inconsequential reasons are my desires.

Now I have come to the most important qualification for boldness. "Herod feared John knowing that he was a just man and holy and observed him . . . and heard him gladly" (Mark 6:20). At this time of history, mysticism and superstition filled society. The ruler of the day recognized John's dedicated lifestyle and feared his holy life. I live in a world of unrighteous living, indifference, political unrest, uncivilized cultural involvement and moral decay. Blindness is everywhere. An upright conscience is hard to find. The Bible says, "blessed are those who hunger and thirst for righteousness for they will be filled" (Matthew 5:6). This is to say that I long for rightness. Craving to be right with God is the priority. "O God, you are my God, earnestly I seek you . . . " (v.1). Rightness with God is based upon his mercy and forgiveness. I do not deserve it but I will admit to the need for cleaning and renewal. Through confession I will be cleansed. My desire, even though I fail at times, is to walk blamelessly and do what is right. Many years ago I took some studies from Moody Bible Institute in Chicago (1960). I learned about the command of God, "Be ye holy for I am holy" (I Peter 1:16). I want to obey that command.

What is a holy life?

It is a life that walks with God (Genesis 5:24).

It is a life that abides in Christ (John 15:4).

It is a life that follow Christ (Colossians 2:6,7).

It is a crucified life and yet a risen life (Colossians 3:1).

It is a life lived in the love of God (Jude 21).

It is a life lived in the faith of the Lord Jesus Christ (Galatians 2:20).

It is a life lived in the Spirit (Galatians 5:25).

It is a life that is not under the dominion of sin (Romans 6:14; 8:2).

How do I obtain a holy life? It is available through unconditional surrender to the Lord Jesus. This means that I yield myself — spirit, soul and body — utterly to God. This involves a simple trust. It is a believing dependence, not an anxious vigilance. I am safe in his hands. Relying upon him will bring assurance of being kept by the power of God through faith (I Peter 1:5).

It involves a soul trust. It is not based upon resolution or religious exercises. It is leaning on Jesus and learning continually of Christ. It is an intense activity of the soul. It involves a sure trust. Fellowship with Jesus will cause me to leap out into action. No matter how stormy the sea, I will triumph in Christ. Since I delight to do his will, I will have peace and joy because I am obeying his Word.

I maintain this life through the empowerment of the Holy Spirit (John 7:38; Acts 1:8). "Except a man be born of water and of the spirit, he cannot enter into the kingdom of God" (John 3:5). Life in Christ starts with belief in his death and resurrection for the forgiveness of sin.

"Whosoever drinketh of the water that I give him shall never thirst, but the water that I give shall become in him wells of water springing up into everlasting life" (John 4:14). This provides a full life in Christ and is accomplished through abiding in Christ. "If any man thirst, let him come unto me and drink. He that believeth on me . . . from within him shall flow rivers of living water" (John 7:37,38). This is the overflowing life. I have been "saved to serve." The extent to which I love Jesus will be revealed in my love for others. It is all through the Holy Spirit. The enablement of the Holy Spirit provides this accomplishment.

The fourth characteristic coming out of John's life was courage. He certainly had courage. Listen to his words in Matthew 3:7, "O generation of vipers, who hath warned you to flee from the wrath to come?" The religious leaders showed up to a baptismal service. The Pharisees believed in being separated from uncleanness. They were very strict in these views. The legal tendency caused them to observe the ceremonial laws. The Pharisees had a lot of influence upon public affairs. They had top spiritual authority. The Sadducees were a great influence on social concerns. The supreme guide to life was the law, not God who gave the law. They devoted their energies to making converts to their own narrow views. John's witness and boldness would finally be the cause to take his life. He had one independent mindset. He would pave the way for Jesus Christ. He was determined to help people onto the straight path of repentance. He was not afraid to sacrifice himself for the righteous cause. Compassion for the people and love for God would drive him forward.

I can have courage that will produce boldness too. I recognize that faith is a total response to God. I have to daily make the decision that the Lord will provide and then rest in his Word.

For this day (Hebrews 3:7,13,15; 4:7) I make the decision of faith to wholly surrender to the authority of God as he has revealed himself in the Scriptures — to obey him. I hereby confess my sin, face the sinful reality of my old nature and deliberately choose to walk in the light, in step with Christ, throughout the hours of this day (Romans 6:16-20; Philippians 2:12,13).

For this day I make the decision of faith to wholly surrender to the authority of God as revealed in the Scriptures—to believe him. I accept only his Word as final authority. I now believe that since I have confessed my sin he has forgiven and cleansed me. I accept his Word of promise to be my sufficiency and rest, at full value, and will conduct myself accordingly (Exodus 33:14; I Corinthians 1:30).

For this day I make the decision of faith to recognize that God has made every necessary provision so that I may fulfill his will and calling. Therefore, I will not make any excuse for my sin and failure (I Thessalonians 5:24).

For this day I make the decision of faith to deliberately receive from God that provision which he has made for me. I hereby renounce all self-effort to live the Christian life and to perform God's service, renounce all sinful activity which only weeps over sin and failure, renounce all sinful praying which asks God to change circumstances and people so that I may be more spiritual, renounce all drawing back from the work of the Holy Spirit within and the call of God without, and renounce all non-Biblical motives, goals and activities which serve my sinful pride.

Having made this confession and these decisions of faith, I now receive God's promised rest for this day (Hebrews 4:1-13). I am going to do my part and I know that God will do his part. I will relax in the trust of faith knowing that in the moment of temptation, trial or need, the Lord will be my strength, sufficiency and boldness (1 Corinthians 10:13).

4

What Victory Does the Gospel Provide?

"Jesus being full of the Holy Ghost . . . was led by the Spirit into the wilderness — being tempted of the devil" (Luke 4:1-13). The wilderness was a barren region between the hill country and the Jordan Valley. Jesus prepared for this battle by fasting. In the previous Scripture, Luke reminded me that Jesus is the Son of Man and the Son of God, born into this world identified with the needs and problems of mankind and yet God.

Even the enemy admits that Jesus is the Son of God. "If thou be the Son of God" (v. 3,9). This is an affirmation by Satan. The fact of Jesus' deity was the basis for the first of the three temptations. Jesus has exposed the tactics of the enemy and how I can overcome when I am tempted. Christ has to be first in everything or he is first in nothing (Matthew 6:22). There are no shortcuts in the Christian life and there is no easy way to spiritual victory and maturity. Jesus met each temptation as a man. He quoted Scripture each time "it is written" (Luke 4:4) (Deuteronomy 8:3; 6:16; 10:20).

I have learned that the Scriptures do work. A life in Christ will experience trials but I can be secure in meeting those challenges. The testimony of Jesus is found in these words, "Jesus returned in the power of the Spirit" (4:14). He was constantly and consciously yielded to the Holy Spirit (John 3:34). Having the power of the Spirit confirms that "God was with him" (Acts 10:38). He is the Son of Man (Luke's gospel) and Son of God (John's gospel). Jesus Christ is my God and Savior (1 Timothy 1:1; Titus 2:13).

His work was accomplished through the power of the Spirit (4:14). "He taught" (4:15) in the Spirit. The Olivet Discourses (Matthew 24:1-15-46) form Jesus' major sermon and his most prophetic message of the coming of the end of the world (or the present age). The Mount of Olives was a ridge of hills east of Jerusalem and separated from it by the Jehoshaphat valley. It covers the whole eastern side of the city of Jerusalem. Three paths led from the valley to the summit. From this place, he could look down on the temple courtyards.

Three questions have been asked by the disciples. "When shall these things be?" (Matthew 24:3). This question refers to the destruction of the temple. Jesus' message includes a prediction of the imminent fall of Jerusalem (A.D.70) and he also goes far beyond to the future during which the "times of the Gentiles" will continue until the end of the Great Tribulation. His sermon is divided into four sections (Matthew 24:4-14; 15-28; 29-31; 32; 25-51). Keep in mind that this was a message given to Jews by a Jew about the future of the Jewish nation. It's a time of tribulation and judgment. God will pour out his wrath on the nations of the world. Satan produces his masterpiece, the Antichrist. He moves into the Jewish temple and proclaims that he is God (2 Thessalonians 2:3,4; Revelation 13). The Antichrist will cause a living statue of himself to be put into the temple and his associate (the false prophet, Revelation 10:10) will cause the whole earth to worship it. Jesus called this statue "the abomination of desolation" (Matthew 4:15). During this period, God will care for his people (v.22). Armageddon (Revelation 16:13-16; 19:11) will happen, Satan will be defeated, the enemies of Jesus will be destroyed and Jesus will establish his kingdom (Revelation 19:11; Zechariah 12:7; 13:1).

"What shall be the sign of thy coming?" (Matthew 24:3). I will give a list of signs taken from Matthew's gospel. There will be religious deception (24:4-5). There have been many false prophets and false Christ's. The final world dictator will lead the nation astray. He is the great peacemaker turned liar. There will always be wars when sinful humanity is present. Famines, international distress, starvation, terribly high prices for food (Revelation 6:6) will cause death, wars and famines. Distress will cause epidemics that will continue to bring death.

Religious persecution (24:9) and acceleration of murders will continue. Christians have always been hated by the world. All nations will be involved. Worldwide chaos (24:10-13), betrayal of one another will be common lack of loyalty in marriages, homes and nations, lawlessness will abound (v.12) and worldwide preaching (24:14). God will choose and seal 144,000 Jewish evangelists who will carry the kingdom message to the ends of the earth. The key thoughts to remember are these things will increase and intensify as the time of Jesus' coming draws near. The Lord's admonition is to not be terrified. I have a loving Father who works all things "after the counsel of his own will" (Ephesians 1:11).

"When will the end of the world come?" (Matthew 24:3). "Immediately after the tribulation" (Matthew 24:29). Cataclysmic events will accompany Christ's return. A visible manifestation will mark his gradual return (Acts 1:11). The "clouds of heaven" indicate that Christ will come from heaven to the earth (2 Thessalonians 1:7-9). Let's keep in mind that day that "no man, not even the angels of heaven, but my Father only will know when he will come" (Matthew 24:36). Noah's day illustrates the condition of humanity at the time of Christ's return (Matthew 24:37). Briefly I have answered the three questions. As I have, my challenge has been in Christ's closing admonitions (Matthew 24:32-25:51). I don't have to be caught unaware of his coming. No surprise!

Increased nationalism may be one of the signs of the end time (Matthew 24:32-35). Increased self-absorption may be one of the signs of the end time (Matthew 24:36-42). Increased deception may be one of the signs of the end time (Matthew 24:42-44). I don't know when Jesus will return for his church. I have to be alert, watchful and faithful. I am grateful that I am not appointed to wrath but to salvation when Jesus Christ appears (1Thessalonians 1:10; 5:9-10). I will certainly go through tribulation (John 16:33; Acts 14:22), but not the tribulation. I am going to heaven. When Jesus Christ takes his church to heaven, he will sit upon his judgment seat and judge his own people.

He will not judge my sins because they have already been judged on the cross (Romans 8:1), but he will judge my works and will give rewards to those who have earned them (I Corinthians 3:9-15). The basis of the reward will be on being obedient or disobedient. I must be a bright light for Jesus. I am challenged to watch, witness and work. I will then receive a reward.

His work was accomplished through the power of the Spirit (4:14). He prophesied in the Spirit. A prophet is one who is divinely inspired to communicate God's will to his people and to disclose the future to them. Pouring forth the declarations of God is the designated purpose of a prophet. The Scriptures presents predictions as a manifestation of God's power and is a response to man's needs.

Jesus Christ was the appointed mediator between God and man. His work was the fulfillment and consummation of the ancient prophetical, priestly function. He began to discharge this function on earth and continues to discharge it in heaven. He is the perfect revealer of the counsel and will of God for the salvation of sinners (Deuteronomy 18:15).

His work was accomplished through the power of the Spirit. He performed miracles (Luke 4:30). He has supernatural power. The Lord's message of grace was a blow to the Jewish exclusivism. They became so angry that they took action to kill Jesus. There are a lot of congregations today that want gracious words but don't want to face the truth (John 1:17). A miracle is a "supernatural manifestation of divine power in the external world." Miracles are out-of-the-ordinary course of events. "He passed through" is an unordinary event. Miracles point to something beyond themselves. They indicate the presence of God. In spite of the unbelief of the people in Nazareth, the Scriptures declare that Jesus of Nazareth is God's Son, the Messiah sent to fulfill his promises. The miracles seal the authority that Jesus is a messenger from God (John 2:18,23; 3:2; Matthew 12:38; Acts 14:3; 2 Corinthians 12:12). They are an evidence of his authority. Thomas based his faith on sight.

Christ promises a blessing for those who believe upon hearing instead of upon seeing. The Gospel provides victory for my daily activities through the power of the indwelling Holy Spirit. Jesus is my example.

5

Who Is the Primary Focus of the Gospel?

The Bible says, ". . . they forsook all and followed Jesus" (Luke 5:11). A few days ago, I found a box of recorded sermon tapes of mine. They were preached in the 1980's. I just happened to select a tape to listen to that the title and text were faded on the label. The sermon was a bold witness to what it really means to follow Jesus. This may surprise you but it is difficult to be a disciple of Jesus. Many words describe a Christian, a Christ follower. As I reviewed my message, I had challenged the congregation to sign an agreement promising to be a bond slave of Jesus Christ. The total existence of my being should be the definition of a follower of Jesus Christ. The word 'Christian' is not a religious designation but a spiritual transformation. It is becoming a new creation. It is being born again. It involves an honest, loyal and obedient commitment to Christ. It is being identified with Christ. The Lord said, "My sheep hear my voice, and I know them and they follow me" (John 10:27). This is a picture of a wholehearted follower of Christ. The Scripture says, "If you continue in my word, then you are truly disciples of mine" (John 8:31). It is finding my self-identity in Jesus.

As a Christian, I am a possession of God (Titus 2:14). I belong to Christ. Since I am his possession, I have to be in complete submission (Romans 12:1; I John 3:22; 1 Corinthians 10:31). Submission requires total devotion, devotion requires dependence, dependence requires accountability. I am accountable to the Master in heaven. He is supreme over the physical and moral universe. He is supreme over human history and over all human beings. He is supreme over the living and dead. Everything is evaluated in terms of the Master's pleasure and profit. I am divine property. "For not one of us lives for himself, and not one dies for himself; for if we live, we live for the Lord, or if we die, we die for the Lord. Therefore, whether we live or die, we are the Lord's" (Romans 14:7,8). It all comes down to "whatsoever you do in word or deed, do all in the name of the Lord Jesus" (Colossians 3:17). It is the testimony of Psalm 23 — "The Lord is my Shepherd; I shall not want . . . he guides me in the paths of righteousness for his name's sake . . . I will dwell in the house of the Lord forever." I follow the sovereign gracious Master who provides his peace.

6

What Is the Basis of Courage Found in The Gospel?

As I read through the next few chapters of the Gospel of Luke, I discovered some highlights that brought courage in my life. Through Jesus Christ' life, death and resurrection, I am able to experience faith (8:11).

Everybody lives by faith in something or someone. My faith is based upon Jesus Christ and the Word of God. "Faith comes by hearing and hearing by the Word of God" (Romans 10:17). In one of Jesus' parables, the sower is Jesus Christ. The seed is the Word of God. It must be planted to work. The human heart is like soil. If it is prepared properly, it will produce a fruitful harvest. I have to be watchful in what I allow to enter my heart. Will it be worthy and make me better? What about the challenge to continue in the Word? My faith has to grow. This takes determination. I also have to weed out anything that hinders my spirituality. The evidence of spiritual growth is fruit bearing. I want to reach others for Christ. I want to develop a solid character. I want to praise the Lord (Hebrews 13:5).

I remember in my childhood that I would work all year long to save enough money to buy a New Testament each summer at a Bible Conference that my family attended. It was my privilege to sit three rows from the front of the tabernacle to hear some of the best preachers of the day. At that young age, I learned a lot and they became my heroes. In my youth, I watched them and I appreciated their dedication to the Lord, especially in their conversations I happened to listen to. In my young adulthood, I would buy the books the preacher-teachers would write. These books would become a treasure of great resources as I grew in Jesus Christ. In my adulthood as a preacher myself, I would spend time at several different conferences and outline sermons in preparation for the whole year. Hearing, reading, keeping, obeying and applying the Word would bring courage.

Courage is provided through faith. Faith produces character, character creates spiritual attitude, spiritual attitude will develop wise values, wise values will cause biblical decisions, biblical decisions will result in blessings. As a believer, I live with eternity in view (1 Timothy 6:17). I will get into trouble with the world. I am the salt of the earth and light of the world (Matthew 8:13-16). Sometimes the salt stings and the light exposes sin. One of the first verses of Scripture I learned was Matthew 6:33, "Seek ye first the kingdom of God and his righteousness and all these things will be added unto you." My life has been blessed because my heart is right. I have to practice the beatitudes because the condition of the heart is what counts. Faith, blessings and prayer will provide courage for daily living. Jesus gives the example of prayer for me. He prayed at his baptism (3:21). He chose the twelve through prayer (6:12). When the crowds increased, he prayed. He prayed at the confession of faith of the twelve and at his transfiguration. He often prayed alone. Effective prayer is the provision for every need and the solution for every problem. My pattern for prayer (11:2-4) is the "Lord's Prayer" (Matthew 6:9-15). I have practiced reciting it every day with my own prayer integrated into it. In knowing the Word of God, I will discover the will of God. I have to learn to experience spiritual discernment in knowing his will and then I can bring my requests to him (11:3-4).

7

What Part Does the Heart Have in the Gospel?

Compassion has been defined as "your pain in my heart." In the next few chapters, Jesus is confronted with the miseries of a dying servant, a grieving widow, a perplexed prophet and a repentant sinner and he helped them all. Jesus is busy ministering to many. His helpers have been sent out. Many miracles are performed. He teaches his disciples three basic lessons about his person, his sacrifice and his kingdom. His life reveals that discipleship is a daily discipline. To follow Jesus is a step at a time and a day at a time. As I look at my life, I pray that I have been a joy to Jesus Christ and not one that is breaking his heart. I continue to be challenged as I commune with him. I am his ambassador sent to represent him in this world and to look for opportunities to show mercy in the name of Christ. Through Jesus' heart he warns his disciples concerning hypocrisy, covetousness, worry, carelessness, discernment and diligence. This is an age of worry. Few legal contracts or guarantees are available. Living faith is the answer. Worry is destructive and it will strangle me. It is deceptive and it gives a false view of life, of itself and of God. There is a difference between making a living and making a life.

When the word of the Lord tells me to love God with my heart, soul and mind, that includes my whole self. The heart is the eyes for seeing spiritual reality. It is where understanding resides and is the origin of spiritual discernment. It is particularly influential in shaping a person's sense of spiritual identity. "Living from the heart Jesus gave me" is a phrase that brings identity together with the spiritual reality of who I am. It is a term that says God designed me to be a particular kind of person with characteristics uniquely my own. When I am living from the heart Jesus gave me, I am being the person he specifically designed. Living this way includes the soul (where the emotions are) and the mind (where the thinking takes place).

Living from my heart is not simply doing what my emotions tell me. That would be folly. Living from my heart means that there is an inner directive which, if governed by the Spirit of God, keeps me on a path that is spiritually attuned to who I am and how God is leading. When my heart is focused on God, I see who I am and what I am to be doing.

The Word of God reminds me that my heart is desperately sick and I need God for healing. The heart from Jesus is a reborn heart, a heart where the Christ resides. There are many references to a transformed heart throughout Scripture. One passage is in Ephesians where the apostle Paul is praying for the new believers. "I pray that out of his glorious riches he may strengthen you with power through his spirit in your inner being, so that Christ may dwell in your hearts through faith" (Ephesians 3:16,17). God wants to live in my heart. When he is there, I will experience a freedom to be the person he created.

It has been said that God is not the great magician, he is the great physician. That saying addresses a question which I need to think about clearly on whether fixes from God are always "quick." People seek the quickest way out of pain which is understandable. Pain, of course, demands immediate attention. A more mature approach, however, is to seek God's redemption in the middle of the pain and ask him to bring healing into my wounds which can be a slower process. God does his work in me pointing me toward wholeness, even while I am in pain. But it is not simply his work, it is my work too. It takes maturity and tenacity on my part to achieve wholeness, and that means persistently dealing with my pain.

There may be times I will not get to a place where I can be free from pain, but I can still experience God's amazing redemption. An often-quoted passage in 2 Corinthians 12 describes how the apostle Paul learned an important lesson. When he was stuck in a tormenting problem which did not go away, even though he pleaded with the Lord three times, he got an answer he was not looking for. God works through weakness. What a profound discovery: he learned to delight in weaknesses, in insults, in hardships, in persecutions and in difficulties. The good news of the gospel is that God wants to be with me in the middle of my struggles. That is precisely when he exercises his strength through me. Paul learned to let God be in charge and to stop asking God to end his hardship. God's strength flowed through him because Paul stopped trying to be in control. He let God take over and God was able to use him more effectively. Paul could delight in suffering because he found it is an opportunity for God's strength to work through him.

Central to the Christian experience is an unchanging belief that God is at work in all things for the good of those who love him and that means all things (Romans 8:28). He is particularly active at work in life's chronic issues.

The time-honored Christian approach to pain and wholeness involves my activity as well as God's. His work in me is to bring redemption to all the traumas which have broken me; my work is to strive for maturity as I progress to wholeness. The word 'redemption' is sometimes difficult to understand simply because it is used in so many contexts. Redemption is God bringing good out of bad, leading me to wholeness and to experience God's amazing power.

The biblical understanding of wholeness is described in the first chapter of James. I am instructed there to consider it pure joy whenever I am in the middle of suffering because that will lead to wholeness. Suffering tests my faith and builds my endurance to that I can be mature and complete — whole. James cautions that I must ask God for wisdom during this stormy process. It takes total faith to believe that God will take me through the storms or I will not be able to "receive anything" from God because I remain "double-minded" (divided) (verse 8). Wholeness comes as I let him lead me through the storms. I am to welcome suffering because it brings down the walls in my fragmented life so that I can become mature and complete. Redemption comes from honestly addressing pain and capturing strength from every pain-filled experience. Suffering will be there but so will God's redemption, leading to maturity and wholeness — a process which takes time but is well worth it.

How Does Jesus Show His Compassion in The Gospel?

Luke emphasizes the humanity of Christ. Luke includes more than the other Gospels about women, children, the home, the Holy Spirit, prayer and praise. As the Son of Man, Jesus has experienced my grief and sorrow. He is able to meet all my needs. Discipleship is serious business. Am I devoted to Jesus? What about the falsehoods shared in Chapter 14? Jesus was fully aware of what was in men's hearts (John 2:24-25). Do I know what is in my heart? Jesus knows me and he cares. He does not compromise his position for mine but welcomes me in my foolishness and ignorance. He forgives me and accepts me (chapter 15). He teaches spiritual values. I am a steward of the Gospel (1 Thessalonians 2:4). He has committed the treasures of his truth to me (2 Corinthians 4:7). I must guard this treasure and invest it in the lives of others. I have to give an account. He will command and reward me (chapter 16). In chapter seventeen, Jesus prepares me for the future with forgiveness, faithfulness, thankfulness and preparedness.

Jesus continues to share his compassion. He seeks the lost. Faithful obedience brings rewards. I am praying that faithfulness will be found in my life. Dr. Luke opened his gospel with the angels' announcement of "peace on earth" but now the theme is "peace in heaven" (2:14). In the next few chapters Jesus steadfastly set his face to go to Jerusalem (9:51). Denial, dejection, dedication, determination and deliverance are words that declare what is about to take place. I have discovered their meaning in Christ's life, crucifixion, resurrection, ascension and in Pentecost. They provide choice, cleansing, enablement, deliverance and comfort.

Biblical Christianity is first of all the person of Jesus Christ. All areas of life must revolve around him. The final authority is the revelation of God. To experience real living, I must accept and obey the will of God. Jesus Christ is to have preeminence in all things. Christianity is not an institution, not a list of rules, not a religious experience and not a certain type of service. It revolves around a person, Jesus Christ the Son of Man and Son of God. I want to give Jesus his rightful place. The Gospel has to do with Jesus Christ, his death, burial and resurrection and the Scriptures. Jesus Christ declared that he was the truth. All wisdom and knowledge find their source in him. Without him, I can do nothing. Genuine Christianity starts with accepting the fact that Christ died to deliver me from the guilt and power of sin. I must repent of my sins and believe in him as my Lord and Savior. Without making this decision of faith, I am condemned, I am rejected by Christ and I am eternally lost. Many years ago I responded with the verse "Believe on the Lord Jesus Christ and thou shalt be saved . . . " This is the promise of God. With that response of obedience, I have been described with these words; saved, adopted, begotten, redeemed, forgiven and justified. I am complete in him and this means I am a finished product. I have received spiritual cleansing and I have been made alive. I have been forgiven and have been justified. I have freedom from Satan. Jesus Christ has provided a choice. I have become a new creation in Christ Jesus.

In his crucifixion, Jesus Christ provided a cleansing from the power, influence and effect of my sinful nature. This nature is called the "old man" (Romans 6:6, Ephesians 4:22). In Christ's death, as my representative Jesus Christ brought my fallen nature under the judgment of God. I am now free from the sinful nature. I possess it and I can feel defeated by it, but I don't have to be (Romans 6:6-22).

In his resurrection, Jesus Christ provided enablement. What does it mean to experience the power of the resurrection in daily life? (Philippians 3:10). I can live with spiritual virtue, grace and power. Instead of discouragement, bitterness and selfishness, I may have love, confidence and hope. The practical benefits are endless.

In his ascension, Jesus Christ provided deliverance. He is my forerunner to heaven. He is my intercessor and I also have legal authority over Satan. I am seated in the heavenlies with Jesus Christ (Ephesians 2:5-6). Daily deliverance from Satan is possible, but I have to guard against him and not allow him some sinful opportunity (Ephesians 4:27).

At Pentecost, Jesus Christ provided the comforter. The Holy Spirit has convicted me of my sinful and lost condition. Through repentance and faith, he has brought me to the new birth. He has provided protection and preservation. I have become a member of the body of Christ (Romans 8:9). I have become the temple of the Holy Spirit (1 Corinthians 3:16-17; 6:19). Through the comforter-helper, I am able to grow in freedom from the sinful nature. I am assured of becoming successful in my eternal life walk. I am now able to live a meaningful life through Christ's compassion. It will continue through my thirst for him, coming to him and drinking of him in faith. As I submit to God and his word, as I practice obedience and I trust him, I will experience the abundant life (John 10:10).

9

Jesus Christ Deity

Who is Jesus Christ?

I have discovered that as I acknowledge that Jesus is the Son of God, living within his authority is available. Jesus Christ is the ultimate personality of the universe. "In the beginning" (John 1:1) refers to eternity which preceded all time. Jesus always was. This gives evidence that Jesus has the same attributes of God. The word "with" in the text (1:1) implies association. He is a living intelligent active personality. Jesus Christ the 'Word' has the same character of God, the same work and the very nature of God. He is deity.

Jesus Christ is the life. This refers not only to conscious existence but of the life of God. Spiritual vitality originates with God and that lifts man out of sin to himself. Christianity is the indwelling of God into our everyday activities. Jesus Christ is the light and through him, I am given spiritual illumination. He is the original light. He is the source. The word 'world'(1:10) has reference to the material and spiritual environment in which we live. He is independent of it and yet a part of it. The only way I can comprehend is through believing and then he gives understanding. I have discovered that Jesus Christ is God. As I read verse 1 and 2, I realize that they are connected to verse 14. In verse 1 and 2, they speak of the eternal nature and relation of Jesus Christ to God and verse 14 connects him with the world of men. God has expressed himself in human personality that was visible, audible and tangible. He partook of flesh. He belongs to humanity as well as to infinity.

The phrase 'dwelt among us' (1:14) means that Jesus Christ camped among us. His stay was temporary. God has come into our daily life. When observation, confession and personal appropriation of the truth take place, he becomes my live-in companion.

No one has ever seen God. The 'only begotten' are words of affirmation that Jesus is deity. He is the revelation of God. Either I accept or reject this truth. Receiving and believing are equivalent terms. Receiving Jesus Christ and believing brings us into a relationship with God and his family. Belief gives the authority to place us into his family. Jesus Christ communicated God to man. I want to be a witness for Jesus and communicate how humanity can have a relationship with God. I want to be an extended light for him and his love.

Why Follow Jesus Christ?

The witness of John the Baptist gives a good reason to follow Jesus. He said "Behold the Lamb of God" (1:29). These words refer to the Messiah which means the anointed one of Christ. "In him was life; and the life was the light of men" (1:4). "This is the record, that God hath given to us eternal life, and this life is in his Son" (1 John 5:11). Either we have received or rejected the Son of God (John 3:36).

The first disciples are good reasons to follow Jesus (John 1:40-51). Andrew followed Jesus and became the first missionary. He enjoyed a special friendship with Jesus. I need to have the same passion to lead others to Christ like Andrew. Peter followed Jesus and became immovable in his convictions. He failed and yet was restored and became a dauntless leader of the church.

I need to have the same convictions like Peter to lead in the church. Philip did not approach Jesus but waited for an invitation. He was not afraid to share his faith even though he made some mistakes. I need to have the readiness for action like he did. Nathaniel was honest and straightforward. He was also skeptical but curious. In his story, I am challenged to realize that Jesus is always working on people's hearts.

God's grace in my life reminds me of his miracles. They provide a good reason to follow Jesus (2:11). They prove that he can do what he has promised to do. The miracles of Jesus confirm his nature, his teaching and his claims. They are a logical expression of his deity.

Did you hear about how Jesus saved a family from social embarrassment? I am sure you have heard about the water being changed to wine. Wine was the normal drink of the people in that day. The Jews diluted the wine with water. The purpose of the miracle is not about alcoholic beverages. Jesus accepted invitations to social events. He entered into the normal experience of life. Jesus had a heavenly time table for everything. We can trust Jesus to do what is right and this miracle was for a few to witness, Mary, the disciples and the servants. This act of kindness revealed Jesus' glory (1:14) and gave a strong foundation to faith. Faith will become deep as you get to know Jesus. Have you experienced his grace in your faith walk?

Did you hear about the father that came to Jesus to intercede for his son who was dying? It does not make any difference who you are whether noble, rich, poor, educated or uneducated, an official or a servant. This father was in desperate need. He believed in the words of Jesus and acted on them. The boy was healed the instant that Jesus spoke, "thy son liveth." Have you been in a crisis in your faith and experienced God's grace? We believe in a God that can heal and provide grace.

Did you hear about the man that was sick for thirty-eight years? He spent his days at a pool that would produce hope for healing of his infirmities. Jesus' grace was seen through his coming to the man, speaking to the man, healing the man and then visiting him later in the temple. We certainly see a tragic hopeless case. The cure was immediate. It happened through the power of his spoken word. What hopeless situation are you with your faith? Has God's grace been experienced?

Did you hear about the feeding of the five thousand? Jesus faced a huge problem. What was he going to do with all those people? The need was food. They needed to have strength to travel back home after hearing him speak. We learn through the bad and the good things that happen to us. One of the disciples found a little boy who had a small lunch. Jesus took the boy's lunch, blessed it, broke it and handed it out to his disciples and they fed the whole crowd. Jesus multiplied the food. Whenever there is a need, give all that you have to Jesus and let him do the rest. Are we thankful to Jesus for the provision he has given? Do not complain about what you don't have but be thankful for what you do have. Let your eyes see his grace at work.

Did you hear about the storm? Sometimes we are caught in a storm of our own making because we have disobeyed Jesus. Sometimes storms come because we have obeyed the Lord. We can be sure that our Savior will pray for us, come to us and deliver us. Jesus walked on the water. He stilled the storm and the boat was instantly on the other shore. I wonder how many people want Jesus as Savior and Lord. How many people want Jesus as healer and provider? How many people want Jesus to rescue them from problems? When the storms of life have come, have you witnessed his grace?

Did you hear about the man that was blind? I am told that in the United States somebody goes blind every twenty minutes. His eyes were opened to see but most importantly, his heart was opened to the Savior. He was born blind. He had never seen the beauty of God's creation on the faces of his loved ones. He was a beggar by trade. Jesus Christ is God but he is also man. The blind man became a witness for Jesus Christ's claims. He discovered that Jesus came for salvation but the result of his coming was condemnation of those who would not believe. His grace makes it possible for me to believe.

Did you hear about Jesus raising somebody from the dead? The person was in the grave four days. Death is man's last enemy, but Jesus Christ has defeated this horrible enemy totally and permanently. In every miracle, there is a human need met and a spiritual truth delivered. His credentials prove his deity. There is no guarantee that we will be sheltered from the problems and pains of life. Jesus is the master of every situation. We must live by faith and not by sight. In Psalm 5:1-3 we find a great promise. Look it up and memorize it. God's grace is seen. Spiritual growth is not automatic. In Jesus' miracles, we are taught to believe his Word. The grace of God provides the way for us to live it out.

The miracles have given evidence of his power. The promises have revealed his grace in action. I am sufficient in all things because of Jesus Christ. Whatever the past, present or future brings into my life, I will experience his grace.

Spiritual transformation gives a good reason to follow Jesus. He knows if we believe or not. He knows the heart of man and can evaluate our faith. What is spiritual transformation? It is the internal change (I Corinthians 5:17) of a person's nature through God's grace. Faith is the process for Jesus to enter and dwell in our hearts (Ephesians 3:17). There should be no confusion, camouflage, cover-up or stumbling.

In Jesus' own words, he declares what the gospel is all about and gives us an explanation. He says that we cannot enter the kingdom of God without becoming a new person. A complete change is compared to a rebirth. The natural man cannot enter into God's kingdom. The word in the text 'cannot' (3:5) implies incapability rather than prohibition. Spiritual transformation has to take place. How can change take place? The pattern of life is set. Physical or psychological change is not the question. It has to do with the spiritual side of man. Jesus gives us these words, "except one be born of water and the Spirit, he cannot enter into the kingdom of God" (John 3:5). In the word 'water,' I discovered that acknowledgement of repentance and cleansing is necessary. A complete turn-around in body, soul and spirit is necessary. To explain the word 'Spirit,' Jesus illustrates by using the word 'wind.' The wind's origin is undiscoverable but whose presence is manifested. Nobody can deny its existence. To be born by the Spirit means that the origin of life cannot be defined but its actuality can be seen by all.

How do I experience this new nature? Jesus continues and says that new birth is a direct result of faith in his death and resurrection power. Jesus gives God's attitude and purpose toward the world. He 'loved us' (3:16) are words of the will rather than emotion. Belief is obedience to the voice of God; disobedience is unbelief. Belief is defined as commitment to authority rather than passive opinion.

We can come to Christ as a learned inquirer. We can come in an attitude of indifference. We can come as a result of desperation. Accept God's love and place your trust in his Son and be spiritually transformed.

What Should Be Included in Worshipping Jesus Christ?

In Jesus' conversation with the Samaritan woman, he gives the true definition of worship (John 4:24). It is found in her heart relationship with God. Many things can be said about this conversation. Much time could be spent on the words, "He must needs pass through Samaria." The use of the word "must" is not based on geographical necessity nor social pressure but a compulsion to seek a lost sheep. The time of day was important. Jesus would be weary and ready to rest. His request was a complete surprise. He asked a Samaritan for water. Jews and Samaritans did not mix together. Jesus gets into the spiritual side of the conversation which was water that is tied to eternal life. He turned her life inside out before her very eyes. He said that to worship God must be done through his Spirit and on the basis of truth. In his conversation with the woman, he would overcome the obstacles of indifference, materialism, selfishness, moral sin and religious prejudice, ignorance and indefiniteness. Through it all, he led her straight to the beginning of an active faith.

In my study of this Scripture, I was challenged to worship with the right attitude. The Samaritans took as much of Scriptures as they wished and paid no attention to the rest. I have discovered that one of the most dangerous things in the world is a one-sided Christianity. It is very easy to accept and hold to certain truths that suit us and disregard the rest. I think to worship in the right way requires that I know what I believe and why I believe it. In this passage, I found these profound words, "God is a spirit and they that worship him must worship him in spirit and in truth" (John 4:24). This is very important to me because it will take me from the present to eternity and eternity to an unending life with

Jesus Christ. A Holy Spirit stimulated vitality will be experienced.

Worship requires approaching God with the whole person. The emotional response is important but that response has to be thought out. My hope is built on solid ground. Real faith is not founded on fear of what might happen if we leave God out of the picture of life. It is a love for God in gratitude for what he has done.

Worship requires the spirit of man to be motivated. The other parts (physical, psychological) will vanish. It is through my spirit that I become intimate with God. True worship is not to come to a certain place. It is not to go through a certain ritual. It is not even to bring certain gifts. It is when my invisible part meets with God. It may be beyond my understanding and it may be full of wonder and amazement.

Worship requires love. The Bible says, "Love the Lord your God with all your heart and with all your soul and with all your mind" (Matthew 22:37-38). Jesus Christ becomes the priority in life. My entire being is activated.

Worship requires spending time with God. I must focus on him. Am I God-conscious? He is always conscious of me. He will never leave me nor forsake me (Deuteronomy 31:6). I initiate God-consciousness through praying, praising, reading the Bible, thoughtful meditation, etc.

Worship requires sensitivity to God. Have I practiced the presence of God? The process begins with belief. "Everyone who sees the Son and believes in him" (6:40). God works through faith and faith is provided as a gift (Romans 12:3; Ephesians 2:8,9). When I believed in Jesus (John 1:12), I received the gift of faith (Ephesians 2:8,9). Faith is the ability to choose to fellowship with God, to obey him, to love him and to acknowledge him in all areas of life through complete submission and aggressive trust.

Through faith I have been forgiven (Acts 26:18). I have a living relationship with God (Romans 1:17). I have been justified (Romans 5:1). I have a life indwelt by God (Galatians 2:20).

12

What Does It Mean to be Selected by God?

"Jesus said, . . . no man can come unto me except it was given unto him of my Father" (6:65). Worship includes selection (John 6:65). When I was a little boy, I sang in a trio. A favorite song discovered for us to sing was entitled "His Very Own." It had three major phrases in it which would provide three short solos for the triplets "chosen by the Father, purchased by the Son and sealed by the Spirit." I am grateful that I have been chosen. This doesn't mean that I merit it. Through God's grace, I have received Jesus Christ as my Savior.

As I began to read through the Gospel of John, I found several verses to verify this truth. Sometimes I think I would like to say that I chose to follow Jesus. I did, but it puts more authority to the subject if I can say that God the Father chose me instead. I became aware of God and his call through the Scriptures, my parents, church leaders, books, songs and preachers. My heart-emotions and mind will make a decision to trust Jesus Christ. I may not understand but I do not really have to. It's who I have trusted in that counts. "Ye have not chosen me but I have chosen you" (John 15:16,17).

I have been enslaved to sin (total depravity) and unable to believe apart from God's empowerment. (Romans 3:1-19, Ephesians 2:1-3, 2 Corinthians 4:4, 2 Timothy 1:9). It is through God's drawing power that I have received Jesus Christ. I have chosen to come to Jesus and God will not turn me away (Romans 10:11-13). The absolute sovereignty of God is the basis of Jesus' confidence. It is also my guarantee and security of salvation. In his sovereignty, I have been drawn to him. My responsibility in salvation is to believe through faith. God's responsibility is to draw me to him. The infinite mind of God is at work whether I understand it or not. The Father has given certain people to Jesus Christ. How do I find out if I am one of them? The answer is by coming to Jesus. I have free will and can choose to come, and I have Jesus' words that he will not turn me away.

God the Father not only created me but has a plan for my life. A part of his work was to impress upon my heart to come to him. "This is the work of God that ye believe in him whom God hath sent" (John 6:29). The work is not something I do for God but it is the act of receiving what God has done for me. I have discovered eternal life through personally accepting Jesus and his claims.

My whole personality played a part in the decision to follow Jesus. My intellect, will and emotion were moved by the Holy Spirit to choose. It was ultimately his will that made it happen. " . . . the Son giveth life to whom he will" (John 6:29). I am so thankful that the prodding of the Spirit was active in my life. It was God's will that I would become a believer.

It may be a mysterious statement but it is also an encouraging truth when the Scripture says,

"Those whom the Father gave him shall come to him" (John 6:37a). The work and will of the Father makes life meaningful. "Salvation of God is not of him that willeth nor of him that runneth, but of God that hath mercy" (Romans 9:16). Salvation involves both divine sovereignty and human responsibility. The Father gives men and women to the Son but these men and women must come to him, that is believe on him. There is no conflict in God's perspective.

Jesus died for the world (John 3:16; 6:51), for his sheep (John 10:11-15), for the nation (John 11:50-52) and for his friends (John 15:12). Jesus is the sacrifice not for our sins only but also for the sins of the whole world (I John 2:2). I am glad that I have heard his call and have come to him.

What Part Does Conflict Play in Jesus Christ's Ministry?

In the last six months of Jesus' life, he faced many conflicts (John 7:17). It is the longest single section in the Gospel of John. It describes the development of belief and unbelief among the hearers of Jesus. It represents fixed attitudes at war with one another and not just unsettled attitudes. The conflicts include unbelief of the brethren (John 7:3-9), the bewilderment of the people (John 7:10-13), public appearances (John 7:14-19), public confusion (John 7:20,25-32), offer of spiritual life (John 7:37-52), women taken in adultery (John 7:53-8:11), and address to the Pharisees (John 8:12-30).

Interpersonal tensions surround everyday living. I have observed strife, jealousy, angry tempers, disputes, slanders, gossip and arrogance (2 Corinthians 12:21,22). The Bible shares breakdowns starting with Adam and Eve, the first married couple, and their first two sons. Jesus and the Biblical writers were peacemakers. I would like to know how I can be a peacemaker. It starts with Jesus. Peace with God comes when we confess our sins and failure to him, ask him to take control of our lives and expect that he will give the peace which the Word of God promises.

It includes growing in grace and becoming spiritually minded which means yielding to divine control. I have been transformed within and that makes a change outwardly in my behavior. Resolving conflicts involves determination, effort and skill. It is not just going to happen automatically. It demands desire, consistent development and application of such skills as listening carefully, watching, understanding oneself and others, refraining from unkind comments or emotional outbursts and communicating accurately.

I have learned that I have to will to do his will. "If any man will do his will" (John 7:17c). I can handle conflicts in light of his will. I cannot judge on the surface level. "Judge not according to the appearance; it must flow from within with divine direction." (John 7:38).

Conflict involves justice (John 8:24). If I refuse God, there are permanent consequences. Jesus said, "I told you that you would die in your sins; if you do not believe that I am the one I claim to be, you will indeed die in your sins" (John 8:24). A full and abundant life has become reality for me when I trusted in Jesus (John 10:10). What a comparison? To magnify Christ's life is to live with the understanding that he is in me. Therefore, I have to keep in mind whatever hinders my intimacy with him must be dealt with. To die in sin is to die forever separated from being in a love relationship with God. According to Jesus, if we do not believe in him, we will not only die a physical death but a spiritual one as well. In the Bible, the second death is a spiritual one (Revelations 20:6,14). This will result in eternal separation from God. I do not like the word "hell" but this is what Jesus calls the place that all sinners will be separated to eternally.

Hell, was not created for human occupation but rather for the fallen angels — angels who chose to go their own way instead of obeying their creator. (Matthew 25:41). All who reject God's will ultimately will be cast out of his presence and live forever in a conscious state of eternal separation from God in hell. Let's keep in mind that there is a choice. If we choose to reject him freely, we choose to live without him forever.

God does not force his love on me. He is persuasive but never intimidating. He will respect my choice even when he knows the reality could be total separation. Hell, has been established to punish evil. Since God is just, he must judge everyone who has sinned and broken his moral law. People who are unwilling to admit their guilt and ask for forgiveness are heading for justice. God's judgment is always right. Judgment will be according to my deeds (Romans 2:6; Revelation 20:12; Psalm 51:4b). The moral law is based upon the nature of God (Psalm 51:4a). When I sin, I am devaluing the image of God and I sin against God.

Sin is a willful violation of God's law. His salvation to the problem of sin is Jesus Christ. Jesus Christ's blood on the cross has become my eternal shield to protect me from the wrath of a holy and awesome God. I have not refused God's generous offer of an eternal covering of my sin. Rejection is a personal choice. Sin cannot be ignored. It has to be confessed. I hate to say it but everyone who will go to hell has chosen to be there.

Sin is the problem and has caused the wrath of God to act. I was born in sin which means that sin is already present in every human being — rooted — inherited (Psalm 51:5; John 3:6). As I live in this twenty-first century, my heart has searched for an answer to this question, "why don't people turn to God's love rather than face his wrath?" In my discussions, I have discovered blindness, voluntary ignorance, insensibility and pollution.

Sin is the problem and has caused the wrath of God to act. The divine remedy is found in Jesus Christ. The word salvation means Savior (Acts

20:28). The word communicates the thought of deliverance, safety preservation, soundness, restoration and healing. Salvation provides a dismissal and removal of every charge against the sinner. It equips him with eternal life in place of death, with the perfect merit of Christ in place of condemnation. It provides forgiveness and justification in place of wrath.

Conflict involves blindness (John 9:39-40). Miracles have been performed to meet human needs. They also present a spiritual truth. They are existing because they have become Jesus' credentials. In his miracle with the blind man, he used it to be the basis for a short sermon on spiritual blindness. (John 9:39-41).

When I was a little boy, I fell down on the school playground and hurt my eye. One of my eyes came in contact with ice patches from the ground. It caused a period of unrest, worry and concern. I had to wear a bandage on the eye until it healed. At school, I seemed to be a hero, of course, I did make a touchdown playing football on all that ice.

Some students were assigned to me to help me get around. Being in the dark is scary. Through God's help, I made it through the experience and can see alright. Spiritual darkness is a greater concern. The verse that stands out in this story for me in regard to blindness is "For judgment came I into the world that they that see not may see, and that they that see may become blind" (v.39). The miracle became a parable. A parable is a story or principle that conveys a meaning indirectly by the use of comparison. It's a dark saying, a proverb.

The miracle illustrated the consequences of belief and unbelief. Persistent faith brought healing and progressive enlightenment. The unbelief of the Pharisees began with misunderstanding both of the law and of the person of Jesus. The law was for them a tradition to be kept and not a living voice. The result of this attitude was a prejudice that blinded the Pharisees to anything but their own preconceived opinions which made them ignorant of the full truth. Pride prevented them from learning anymore and their bigotry caused them to drive Jesus away.

John 9:39 does not contradict 3:16-17. Jesus came for my salvation but the result of his coming was condemnation of those who would not believe. The religious leaders were blind and would not admit it. Therefore, the light of truth only made them more blind. Look around and you will see the people that are blind and do not want to see. As for them, they have knowledge. My heart goes out to them because they are really lost. Jesus calls those people "blind leaders of the blind." (Matthew 15:14). They have become blind through their pride, self-righteousness, traditions and false interpretation of the Word of God. Ignoring the evidence caused them to decide to follow their own will.

I have talked to several people that are spiritually blind. I am deeply concerned for them. Some think that:

God is unknowable.

God doesn't exist.

It is not crucial to understand.

They are the judge of human events.

Self and meism are the way.

Parts of the Bible are denied.
The Bible is the Word of God but other books are equal to it.
Salvation must be obtained through good works.
God is impersonal.
It is foolish to think that there is only one way to God.
There is no evil in the world.
There are too many contradictions in the Bible.
The Bible is not relevant.

Jesus is the light of the world (John 8:12; 9:5). The only people who cannot see the light are blind people, those who refuse to look and those who make themselves blind. "If any man wills to do God's will, he shall know of the doctrine" (John 7:17). I am glad that I am not blind. "The path of the just is as the shining light that shineth more and more unto the perfect day" (Proverbs 4:18).

14

What Does the Abundant Life Refer To?

I can enjoy an abundant life in the Lord (John 10:9,11). I have the assurance of a full and free life. Jesus not only gave his life for me but he has given his life to me right now. Jesus has delivered me from bondage. I have salvation in him. The word "saved" means delivered safe and sound. I can rest on what he says because of what he has done. He died for me (John 10:11-13). Five times in this sermon, Jesus clearly affirmed the sacrificial nature of his death. He died as a substitute, willingly laying down his life for me. His dying is efficient only for those who will believe. He also knows me. Knowing means intimate relationship, not intellectual awareness. He knows my name (v,3) and knows my nature.

(Psalm 23:1,6). He takes up his life again (v.17-18). His voluntary death was followed by his victorious resurrection. He yielded up his spirit to the Father. He voluntarily took up his life and arose from the dead. The Father gave him the authority in love. If I don't believe, I will die in my sins. I am able to live life to the fullest because of what Jesus has done for me.

An abundant lifestyle involves living with the resurrection power. I have made the decision to follow the Lord wholeheartedly. I have had to learn to organize my life around the promise of God. I am not to hold anything back. I am to live by the absolutes of the Scripture and choose to keep to my convictions. I am to accept challenges and work my way through them. I am to live with unlimited faith that God has provided.

An abundant lifestyle involves gratitude. I have to develop a heart of appreciation. My conversation needs to be positive. Any negatives should push me forward into a deeper trust. When I get up in the morning, I have to discipline my mind to be thankful. God is gracious and there is always something to be grateful for. The positive list is always longer than the negative. I am thankful for opportunities, health, wife, and my children, grandchildren, friends, etc.

An abundant lifestyle involves praising others for their achievements. Encouragement is the center focus. Reflection on past accomplishments is replaced with helping the younger generation to become successful. One must have a peaceful acceptance of the reality of life and the adventure of new things around the corner and commitment to glorify the Lord Jesus Christ which helps in the adjustments of life.

An abundant lifestyle involves keeping the mind alert and grasping new ideas. There is no idea of stopping the thinking process. The goal-setting and tackling of new ideas are always present. Change is not an enemy but a friend. Reading and pursuing new disciplines, keeping current with events of the day and sharing interests with others keeps me moving ahead.

An abundant lifestyle involves seeing the big picture. Reading the daily headlines does not disturb me. I know who is in charge. My energy is flowing through the blood of Jesus. My life is not crippled with todays' blindness and depression. There is a sense of confidence because God has the blueprint for life.

15

How Does Feeling Good About Jesus Christ Work?

In my childhood, I learned the shortest verse in the Bible, "Jesus wept" (John 11:35). I heard the story about a family that had experienced sickness and then death. I discovered the emotions involved in the story. Emotion is a psychological state that arises spontaneously. It is often accompanied by physiological change which is a feeling of sadness, anger, joy, sorrow, reverence, hate and love.

Our feelings are important. We cannot neglect their influence on our lives. Feelings are neither right nor wrong and they are simply there. What I do with a feeling makes it right or wrong. Feelings are vital and necessary in our makeup as human beings. I have to understand them. Denial will result in emotional illness.

I have had to learn to not trust my senses or my feelings. I don't live on whether it feels good or if it seems right. God has given us his Word to give guidance. I am not led by what is right in my own eyes. I have to exercise faith in God's Word and not human reason regardless of the false signals sent out by my senses. Life requires many adjustments in the different transitions that have to be made in life. Following my senses is a gradual process and will result in a habitual choice pattern. A continued reliance upon God is necessary to keep me in a straight and level position headed in God's direction.

I don't remember who said this but it is a good statement, "you do what you do and you feel what you feel because you think what you think." The mind accounts for your ability to think, remember, love, hate, feel, reason, imagine and analyze. The body also responds physically to its direction. The Bible says that I should control my mind. "Guard your heart" (Proverbs 4:23), "take captive every thought" (2 Corinthians 10:5), "temptation begins in my mind" (James 1:13). Believe it or not, the mind can be controlled but it takes discipline and hard work (Hebrews 12:11).

The next three thoughts come from my first book entitled, "Thoughts to Ponder" published through Torch Publishing Company in 1984. Controlling the mind and my feelings involves the renewed mind. The Bible says, "And be not conformed to this world; but be ye transformed by the renewing of your mind, that ye may prove what is that good and acceptable and perfect will of God" (Romans 12:2). Our minds need to be transformed. Whatever we have learned, we can also unlearn and relearn. It is a wonderful thing to look at the world objectively, yet with hope, faith and love. The renewing of the mind will help us to become more sensitive and alert to our fallibilities, as well to our potentialities and will help us to become less mechanistic and less fatalistic.

We must accept responsibility for our thinking, feelings and behavior. We reject the theory that we are wholly determined by our past. Our mental lives need to be based on reason and our spiritual lives need to be based on faith. We are dealing with an objective analysis of our perceptions, thinking, feeling and behavior. It is studying the facts and events (our perceptions) and our emotive feelings. Get the facts, be objective and choose the feeling you really want to experience. The Bible says, "for as he thinketh in his heart, so is he" (Proverbs 23:7).

Controlling the mind and my feelings involves taking charge. The Bible says, "we are troubled on every side yet not distressed" (2 Corinthians 4:8). In reading this text, we can discover for ourselves that a tremendous choice over our feelings and learning to look above and beyond ourselves is possible. God says take charge of your life through the Holy Spirit's guidance.

The basic problem that most people experience is that they operate more on feelings than on reason. They would rather rely on their sense organs than their mind. Everything that goes into the mind must be evaluated with objective thinking. Our minds are filled with memories, rational and irrational belief, ideas, attitudes, prejudices, biases and fantasies. We are prone to misinterpret, misjudge and misunderstand, therefore, we suffer.

The Bible says, "Beloved, believe not every spirit, but try the spirits whether they are of God . . . every spirit that confesseth that Jesus Christ is come in the flesh is of God" (I John 4:1,2). We must feed our minds with the right kind of food. Eating garbage will produce unhealthy results; confusion, doubts, fears, jealousy, anger and hostility. Let us recognize what is wrong and then become firmly committed to change. Let us take charge of our lives by allowing God to work in us.

Controlling the mind and my feelings involves being obedient. The Bible says, "For the weapons of our warfare are not carnal, but mighty through God to the pulling down of strongholds, casting down imaginations and every high thing that exalteth itself against the knowledge of God, and bringing into captivity every thought to the obedience of Christ" 2 Corinthians 10:4,5). This obedience is possible because of what Christ has already done. Because of Christ's victory on the cross, we have a right to evict the thoughts that come from the flesh and the devil.

We must refocus our thought life, not to win the victory, but to receive the victory that has already been won. Only if we understand our authority can our minds be renewed. Receiving Christ as Savior gives us a new nature, but the old thought patterns often continue. In Jesus Christ's name is our authority — let's take charge through him. We must reprogram our minds with God's Word and his Word will increase our faith. Our lives would be changed if we spent twenty minutes with God each day before 9:00 am. It would keep us spiritually refreshed and we would begin each day committing ourselves to God.

The Bible says, "Watch over your heart with all diligence, for from it flow the springs of life" (Proverbs 4:23). We must fill our minds with the wonder of Christ and desire to be like him. We must have verses of Scripture ready to quote at a moment's notice. We must always be ready to combat lies with the truth of God's Word. God himself must be first in our thinking. Do you want to master yourself just so you can have a clear conscience, live a successful life and raise a fine family? Or are you fully committed to living to the praise of God's glory?

God lets us struggle so that in the end we will have a greater appreciation of him. Don't run from him when you fail, but run to him. He's waiting for us to give up our toys and fully surrender our hearts to him. What kind of a relationship do we have with God?

Controlling the mind and my feelings involves being a doer. The Bible says, "But be ye doers of the word, and not hearers only, deceiving your own selves" (James 1:22). Millions of people are needlessly suffering from a wide range of serious afflictions, difficulties and problems, including physical and emotional disorders which are often self-induced and self-maintained. Perhaps as much as 70% of our physical and emotional problems are caused by ourselves.

Everything is well in our churches, communities and country is not at all the truth.

Many leaders are fearfully afraid to stick their necks out, to be disliked, to rock the boat, to upset the status quo, or to lose the support (financial and otherwise) of their followers. Unless people begin to grasp the reality of their lives and begin to appreciate the condition of the world and the task God has set before us, there will be little hope for the future.

The problems are remaining because we have made Jesus Christ fit our thinking, our ideologies, our dogmas, our churches, our customs and we are trying to interpret him from our own so very limited knowledge and experience while rejecting the very foundation of his teaching. We have failed to listen to Jesus Christ who tells us to pray and work, to have faith and reason, to hear and do and to follow his footsteps. The Bible says, "Be a doer of the Word."

What Is Involved in Praising Jesus Christ?

As I come to chapter twelve (John 12:12-16) of the Gospel of John, I am always excited about the "triumphant entry of Jesus into Jerusalem." It is one of the few incidents in Jesus' life reported in all four Gospels. By this action, he presented himself officially to the nation as the Messiah and Son of God. Jesus entered the city on his own time and forced the whole issue in order that it might happen exactly on the Passover day when the lambs were being sacrificed. The Bible says, "Christ our Passover was sacrificed for us" (1 Corinthians 5:7, 1 Peter 1:19). In God's perfect timing, he presented himself to die.

The word "Hosanna" found in this passage means "give salvation now." It was a term of praise. I would have liked to be there waving a palm branch. I believe that he is the Son of God and the Son of Man. He is the supernatural one, the deity, and is a human being and my substitute. I want to give him adoration, admiration and acclamation.

Singing Hallelujah, praising the Lord, should be a natural part of life. Hallelujah, he has brought himself into my presence. I have a promised helper. It is hard to believe that he indwells me. He is only a breath away. I am learning to breathe out my impurities and breathe in his presence.

He has brought happiness. In being sensitive to sin and following his initiative, my roots are becoming grounded. Seeking his kingdom brings joy. Learning to live in his presence brings security. Hallelujah, he has brought victory even when surrounded with helplessness. Learning coping skills are available in Jesus Christ. "It is he that hath made us and we are his" (Psalm 100:3). He created me and I belong to him. Making the adjustment to abide in him is the key.

He has brought comfort during the time that disease entered my death-doomed body. Keep in mind there is the promise of the redemption of the body for which all true believers wait. God has said until then, "I am with you, I will watch over you and I will give you rest" (Genesis 18:15; Matthew 11:28). Those words bring comfort and strength in illness. As I recite his word (Matthew 6, Psalm 23) and reflect on his past answered promises. I can rely on having right-thinking during suffering.

He has brought hope. I hope my praise can be contagious and bring encouragement, exhortation and confident expectation. I am learning to trust in Jesus. He is worth believing. My hope is built on Jesus' name. I regularly recite his names. "He is called wonderful, counselor, the mighty God, everlasting Father and the Prince of Peace" (Isaiah 9:6). I review his names in my mind and I rehearse their meaning. Then I act upon them by being amazed with his wonder and reading his Word to obtain wisdom. He is the mighty God and everlasting Father which gives me confidence because he is sovereign. Peace will be the goal and ultimate reality of praise.

There are many ways to praise the Lord. I praise him when I find pleasure in him. I praise him when I worship him. I praise him when I share his faithfulness. I praise him when I model a Christ-like life. I praise him when I find delight in his Word. I praise him when I get up in the morning and say 'good morning' to him and when I end the day asking him if he had good company with me. I praise him when I say 'I love you for who you are not just for what you have blessed me with.' I praise him when I study and share his Word.

I have used Psalm 150 hundreds of times to introduce my trumpet solos or ensemble performances. I have preached from the text and have taught it in the classroom. I have been reminded of it when I listen to great symphonies. In only six verses, it emphasis thirteen times to praise the Lord. Each word like each note in an overture is very important. When I put it all together, it will show God's majesty, excellence and greatness.

The word 'praise' or 'Hallelujah' means to honor, respect and admire. It is a shout of joy, reverence and gratitude. The word 'Lord' in the Hebrew language means ownership. He is in absolute control. He is the governor of the whole earth and beyond. I have the privilege to praise the supreme one because the 'ye' refers to me. The words "praise God' clarified the fullness of his divine power. His name 'Yahweh' is defined as he is the self-existent one, the supreme personal intelligence, the creator and preserver of all things. The divine trinity is worthy of singing Hallelujah to. He is tri-personal and has the same nature. What a history to behold! God the Father is the creator God; God the Son is the redeemer God and God the Spirit is the sustainer God.

"Praise ye the Lord...praise God in his sanctuary." Just think of it, I am his sanctuary. The church is his dwelling place and I am a part of that body. What a tremendous responsibility and awesome opportunity to praise. Pause for a moment and then say 'thank you' God on your knees.

"Praise him in the firmament of his power." He is not only here and present with us but now he expands his territory to everywhere. Look around, look into the depths of the sea and look up into the heavens. What splendor, what glory, what radiance and what unapproachable light.

Praise him for his mighty acts. God is totally responsible for all creation. His sovereignty concerns his absolute rule and control. It is beyond me to understand but through faith I accept. Think of it, he knows all things, he is all-powerful, he is everywhere-present and we have the duty and right to bow before him in praise and say in humility 'hallelujah.' But he doesn't stop there. He goes further. He says, "praise him according to his excellent greatness." I am on my knees as I reflect on his holiness. As I think of all his knowledge and that he knows how to use it (wisdom), I thank him for my blessings and realize I can count them because of his goodness. His excellent greatness is seen in his grace. I don't deserve it but I have experienced his unmerited favor.

Now I have come to his orchestration--a symphony of praise and a Hallelujah Chorus. The sound of the trumpet reveals the wind instrument that will get my attention. It blasts the heralder's notes of praise. The psaltery and harp reveal the stringed instruments that bring unity and harmony. The timbrel, cymbals, organ pipes and dance will reveal the percussion instruments that will unite all the instruments into a complete voice of praise.

"Let everything that hath breath praise the Lord." God breathed everything into existence. He is the giver of life. He provides the breath to praise. There is no other direction to follow. Every breath I take is given through God's grace. He has given life to the fullest. Every moment of every day I take in air to breath to sustain life. This should be a reminder to praise Him.

What is a Permanent Badge of Discipleship?

Jesus said, "Love one another, even as I have loved you" (John 13:34). Love is a permanent badge of discipleship and a foundation of unity. What is involved with his kind of love? I have to look at his love for his disciples. He said, "I have loved them unto the end" (John 13:1). What was his last demonstration of love? This love is a preview of the meaning of the cross.

His love was freely given. It couldn't be quenched with evil in spite of his full knowledge of the coming betrayal and denial. I have to demonstrate love even if good people don't understand my determination to serve and bad people that bring their criticism, ridicule, harassment and gossip.

His love was given with a submissiveness. Jesus was aware of his exalted powers. He deliberately subjected himself to the needs of his disciples. I am not a victim to the enemy. I have voluntarily given my will to love. My time, energy and gifts are his. He has enabled me.

His love transcended the barriers of social class. He was conscious of his divine origin and of his divine destiny. I am also determined to cross over any class distinction. When my own inadequacies come into the picture, I have to realize who I am representing. I am honored to serve all nationalities, all income brackets, all intellectual levels and all spiritual levels of maturity.

His love is active. Twice it is stated that the supper was interrupted. Jesus took the responsibility to prepare the disciples to eat. Washing their feet was the task. Whatever the task, washing the toilets in the bathroom or dusting the pulpit, I must be willing to take the initiative. Whatever my gifts are, he will provide opportunity to enrich his kingdom.

His love cleansing must be constant. A thorough washing or cleansing took place on the cross through Jesus Christ's blood. This cleansing is a once for all task. The constant cleansing is to remove daily encounters with sin. Every day will bring a time to bow before the Master and to be convicted of sin and to confess.

I want to infect others with the love of Jesus. I know God loves me because the Bible tells me so, but do I really experience his love for me? When I became a father, I discovered what my heavenly Father's love was like even in a most limited way. My nature is to show love by touch, word, time and excitement. I am here. I have time for you. My love is not build on fear or guilt. Jesus said, "Love the Lord your God with all your heart, with all your soul and with all your mind" (Matthew 22:37-38). When was the last time I simply hugged the Lord?

Sometimes I think I am alone. No one really understands me. Then God's Word reminds me that he knew me before he made me (Jeremiah 1:4,5). He is not only sovereign but he intimately knows me. As I digest this truth, it has changed my daily perspective in life. It is an astonishing fact. God treasures me. The Holy Creator sees me as his glorious inheritance (Ephesians 1:18). He anticipates my departure from the earth to be with him. I call him Abba Father.

To experience true love (Jesus' example), I have to spend time pursuing it. My prayer is "earnestly I seek him, I thirst for him, my body longs for him" (Psalm 63:1-5). I am driven by a person within. To experience true love, I have to let Jesus in (Revelation 3:20). I do not have to try harder and I do not have to feed my inadequacies. I do not need to be driven by guilt.

I hold to the truth "Come near to God and he will come near to you" (James 4:8). I have memorized its words and meaning. It has given support and encouragement. It has given peace and joy and a given a spirit of triumph. It has provided love.

To experience true love, I need God to help me love God. The supernatural has to take place. Genuine love is produced through the indwelling of the Holy Spirit. To experience true love, I must start running toward it. My constant focus on Jesus will keep me from sin. Freedom from past guilt, injustice, worry, analyzing and road blocks will be removed. To experience true love, I have to expect trouble (John 16:33), but I also anticipate overcoming.

18

Where Can I Find Comfort in These Days?

The promise of comfort is provided by Jesus Christ, not only in his future return but also in the present with the ministry of the Holy Spirit (14:26). The scene is in the Upper Room where the disciples had gathered. The work of the disciples was about to be shattered. Confusion, bewilderment, anxiety and devastation would transpire. The word "troubled" involves many words to describe their hopelessness. Jesus thinks back to his words, "my soul is troubled" which described his deep horror facing the wrath of God on our behalf.

Jesus' departure would be for their advantage since he was going to prepare a heavenly home for them and would return to take them so that they might be with him. This passage refers to taking believers from earth to live in heaven. I am grateful that his words, "I am the way, truth and life" (John 14:1-6) have brought confidence to my life. As I reflect on the past few chapters of the Gospel of John, I have been given comfort to face tomorrow.

Life involves communication. Jesus communicated God to humanity. He is the "word." The word is a means to communicate God to mankind. The indwelling of God is accomplished through Jesus. I pray that I might be a good communicator of the faith.

Life involves relationships. New relationships bring freshness to life. A relationship with Jesus brings intimacy with God. Building relationships is important. I pray that I might learn to follow Christ's model in making relationships.

Life involves sufficiency. The Scriptures say, "my grace is sufficient." I can rely upon his word. Sufficiency is a sure thing because God is sovereign. He is in charge. I pray that I will learn to be dependent upon Jesus alone.

Life involves transformation. Transformation takes place when I fully accept Jesus' claims and commands. An internal change of a person's nature through God's grace takes place when I believe in Jesus. Faith is the process of Jesus to enter the heart. I pray that I can model the transformation that has taken place in my life.

Life involves worship. This depends upon my heart relationship with God. Worship involves truth and the spirit. Worship requires love, the whole person, my spirit and time. I pray that I can be God-conscious at all times. I have to learn to practice his presence.

Life involves belief. Believing involves faith. I believe in Jesus. I receive the gift of faith. Faith requires complete submission and aggressive trust. It is easy for me to trust Jesus because he is God. He is real and genuine. I pray that I can be confident in my reliance on him.

Life involves selection. Saving faith is a gift of God. It is an act of the will and mind. It is a spiritual union brought about by God himself. He has chosen me. I have responded to that call.

I pray that thanksgiving will always be in my heart. I do not merit his grace.

Life involves conflict. Interpersonal tension surrounds every-day living. Jesus was a peacemaker. Transformation within brings change outward in my behavior. Resolving conflict involves determination, effort and skill. It demands desire, constant development and application. I pray that I will yield my will to Jesus and thus I will think Biblically.

Life involves justice. Consequences of evil behavior will certainly become a part of my life. God loves me and will discipline me because he loves me. Whatever hinders my intimacy with Jesus must be dealt with. I pray that I will choose to live for him and will please him in all my activities.

Life involves blindness. I am speaking of understanding spiritual blindness. The parable is about a blind man that is able to see through Jesus performing a miracle. The miracle illustrates the consequences of belief and unbelief. The Pharisees were blind to their own preconceived opinions and therefore ignorant of the full truth. Christ's coming brought salvation and condemnation. I am thankful that I am not blind and pray that I will be a bright light shining in a world that is blind.

Life involves abundance. Jesus not only gave his life for me in the past, but he has given his life to me right now. I live a full and complete life in him. I am learning to organize my life around his promises. The key is a wholehearted attitude of submission. I pray that every day energy will be in my blood stream because of his blood that was shed for me.

Life involves emotions. Feelings are important. They are neither right nor wrong. What I do with a feeling makes it right or wrong. Life is made up of many transitions. A continued reliance upon God is necessary to keep in a straight, level position. This will lead toward God's direction. Feelings have to be directed through the "renewed mind." I pray that my spirit will lead the way for my soul and my soul will lead the way for my body and that all of me will be yielded to the Holy Spirit.

Life involves praise. Praising Jesus Christ is a natural part of life. I want to give personal adoration to him. I want to give public admiration to him. I want to acclaim Jesus with enthusiasm to everyone that I come in contact with. I pray that happiness, comfort, sensitivity to sin, hope and reverent gratitude will be found in my shout for joy.

Life involves love. God loves me and treasures me. The holy creator sees me as his glorious inheritance (Ephesians 1:18). He anticipates my departure from the earth to be with him. I call him "Abba Father." I pray that the Holy Spirit will produce genuine love in me for him and for the creation that he has made.

Life involves comfort. When my heart is troubled, I only have to review the previous chapters and I will be filled with comfort. I do not live with hopelessness because my hope is in Jesus Christ. I live with eternity and heaven in mind. My testing is found in Jesus who said, "let not your heart be troubled." This is my prayer.

What Does Remaining in Jesus Christ Mean?

The Bible says, "Remain in me and I will remain in you" (John 15:4). The secret of producing fruit is remaining in the vine. To remain in Jesus means that his words remain in me (v.7). Loving Jesus will energize obedience to his commands (v. 9-10). Joy will become a real part of my life and a sense of completeness will follow (v. 11-12). There is confidence that comes with remaining in him because he has chosen me to bear fruit. Love for him and others will be the manifesting factor (v.17). Remaining in Jesus takes dedication and is a developmental process. It moves me from the finite to the infinite while still in a mortal body.

Remaining begins with evaluating my spiritual condition. Limitless building can take place if I am sure of my salvation in Jesus. The Scriptures say, "Examine yourselves to see whether you are in the faith; test yourselves" (I Corinthians 13:5). Am I a new creation in Christ? Has anything changed in my life? How can I be certain I am justified? I can have assurance simply because God can be trusted. I have the testimony through his Word (I John 5:9,12). God says that if I believe on Jesus as my Savior then I am justified. In my earthly life, I have had to accept human testimony. Why shouldn't I accept God's testimony?

Remaining provides an internal assurance. Do I see things differently? The Holy Spirit brings new understanding and views to divine truth. The soul can discern the truth of God. To confess that Jesus is the Christ is to confess the Christ of the Scriptures. The teacher of the Holy Spirit in one's life brings assurance of faith. I have discovered that as I search the Scriptures, it leads to a righteous life. It doesn't mean that I will be sinless. It means an increased dissatisfaction with sin. I am in Jesus Christ because I am desirous to keep his Word. A genuine love causes me to remain and abide in him. Morally, I seek to follow Jesus and be an example to others. As I yield wholeheartedly to the Holy Spirit, he produces the character that is needed. Love is the mark by which the world may know the true Christians. Regeneration will produce love. Love is an attitude which determines what I do.

Remaining continues with participation. To be a follower of Jesus Christ means action, not observation. I need to present my spirit, soul and body to Jesus. It has to take place in that order. The spirit dictates to the soul what to do and the soul tells the body how to respond. The inner man is the spirit. It is the breath of God. It is that part of me that is united to the Holy Spirit. God's Word becomes a part of the inner being, the spirit. By using the Scriptures, spending time in it, memorizing it and meditating on it will cause spiritual growth. The world wants to control the mind but God wants to transform it. The mind is a part of the soul and will change from within. The Holy Spirit changes my mind by releasing power from within. The inner man (spirit) will tell the mind (soul) what to think. The will is united to the mind and tells it what to do. The body is the dwelling place of the Holy Spirit and must be surrendered to the Lord. Yielding body, soul and spirit to the Holy Spirit will keep me abiding in Jesus.

Remaining includes a thorough working knowledge of the Bible. Filling the mind with knowledge without the heart will leave only emptiness. Learning to handle the word of truth correctly is necessary (2 Timothy 2:15). This takes discipline, dedication and discernment. The psalmist shared this reference from the Scriptures: "Thy word is very pure; therefore, thy servant loves it . . . the sum of thy word is truth and every one of thy righteous ordinances is everlasting" (Psalm 119: 140,160). Read the promise, "For as the rain cometh down and the snow from heaven, and returneth not thither, but watereth the earth, and maketh it bring forth and bud, that it may give seed to the sower, and bread to the eater; so shall my Word be that goeth forth out of my mouth; it shall not return unto me void, but it shall accomplish that which I please, and it shall prosper in the thing whereto I sent it" (Isaiah 55:10,11). To the same purpose Jeremiah has written, "Is not my word like as a fire? Saith the Lord; and like a hammer that breaketh the rock in pieces?" (Jeremiah 23:29). We cannot be lazy. Study the Word, apply the Word and be blessed.

20

How Does Remaining in Jesus Christ Involve Prayer?

When I was a teenager, I memorized John 16:24, "until now you have not asked for anything in my name, ask and you will receive, and your joy will be complete." I was very interested in doing God's will. I have always had joy when I had fellowship with him. I wanted to ask and receive. Jesus Christ prepares his disciples for the hatred that will be directed toward them. Persecution is going to be a part of their life. Jesus is going away and he wants to get them ready. The Holy Spirit is going to come and this will bring triumph and not tragedy. The work of the Holy Spirit is to convict or convince. He will convict of sin, righteousness and of judgment. They were taught that the Holy Spirit would guide them into a complete knowledge of all truth. Because of the finished work of Christ, I am able to come to the Father in Christ's name and be heard and responded to. The testimony of Jesus Christ is found in his eternity, his humiliation and his exaltation (v.28). I may experience tribulation in the world but will overcome because I have peace, joy and the privilege to love God the Father through Jesus Christ and the guidance of the Holy Spirit in prayer.

I have learned that if I want something from God I need to just pray. The process has been slow but steady. A condition of getting things is asking for them. After memorizing John 16:24, my mind and heart were turned to Matthew 7:7,8. This would start me on the path in praying in his name. This text says, "Ask, and it shall be given you; for everyone that asketh receiveth; and he that seeketh findeth; and to him that knocketh it shall be opened." Jesus means exactly what he said. He says literally to keep on asking, keep seeking and keep knocking. He is eager to answer my prayers.

To pray in his name involves praying in faith. I have to ask in faith with confidence that I am responding to the Scripture in the correct way (Matthew 9:29). Keep in mind that faith is made up of two parts which are belief and unbelief. Remember the father who came to Jesus and said, "Lord, I believe; help thou my unbelief" (Mark 9:24). His prayer was answered and his boy was healed. Faith can be found between unbelief and certainty. Asking fulfills the requirement of faith. Accept the faith that God has given and grow. As I claim his promises, I will grow. Asking is proof of faith.

To pray in his name involves his will (I John 5:14,15). I have to know him. I have to learn to be submissive to the leading of the Holy Spirit. I am so thankful that the Spirit is my teacher. He is able to give understanding. An honest examination of the Word of God, understanding motives, listening to the Spirit and developing relationships are means in knowing his will. I am not alone — I have a helper (Romans 8:26). The Holy Spirit makes intercession for me. I must simply ask, be sincere and be honest.

To pray in his name doesn't mean that I simply use that phrase at the end of my prayer. It means that what I ask for will please and give honor to the Lord Jesus. Ask things for Jesus' sake. I have to learn to ask for things that Jesus wants. I cannot do that if I do not spend time with him. I believe praying brings me into God's presence. The more I am in his presence, the greater understanding I will have in praying in his will.

As I learn to pray, I realize that I have an enemy working hard to stop my interest in being in God's presence. There is raging at this moment a warfare in the heavenlies between the forces of heaven and hell. That fallen rebel who once sought to establish himself as God now moves ceaselessly throughout the earth, and aided by his loyal followers seeks to maintain control over my mind and heart.

God could choose to disarm and defeat the evil one, but he has sovereignly ordained that he would move through the means of prayer and fasting, to loosen the chains of darkness, to tear down satanic strongholds and to release his supernatural power.

Prayer should become our first and natural response to every circumstance of life. As I learn to ask and expect answers, sometimes my mind will follow another route with these questions: Why is it that God sometimes does not answer my prayers? Is the Bible not true in regard to prayer? Is it impossible for God to answer? The enemy is at work. Do I pray with a selfish purpose? I might ask according to his will but have an inner motive of my own gratification. I have to pray with the supreme nature to glorify Jesus (I Corinthians 10:31). What I am praying for should glorify the Savior's name.

Do I pray with sin in my life? I might be praying in God's will but I have sin in my life (Isaiah 59:1,2). God is holy and cannot be in the same breath with sin. There is a separation that is necessary. I have to practice asking God if there is anything wrong in my life anywhere and to show me what it is, and I will give it up. He will make this known and then confession must take place (I John 1:9). What is displeasing to God needs to be emptied out of my life.

Do I pray with idols in my heart? Idols will stop spiritual power in a person's life. An idol is anything that I put before God: church, family, social position, job, education, reputation, power can all become idols. I must repent and change focus.

Do I pray with an unforgiving spirit? I have to search my heart and bring to light any enmity that may be in my heart toward anyone (Mark 11:25). Have I bitterness toward someone who has wronged me? If I do, I must give it up to the Lord if I am going to experience power. I believe praying releases God's power in my life when I am walking in intimacy with him.

21

What Part Does Remaining in Jesus Christ Have to Do with Intercession?

Praying is a growing process. It has been an exciting journey to talk with my heavenly Father. Jesus Christ has paved the way and the Holy Spirit has brought understanding. I have looked at four responses to prayer: I believe prayer brings me into God's presence, I believe prayer releases God's power in my life, I believe praying develops my fellowship with God, I believe prayer requires my dependence upon God. Each of these thoughts have led me into intercession for others in my prayer life. Jesus said, "Neither pray I for thee alone, but for them also which shall believe on me through their word" (John 17:20).

Praying is an essential part of my life. It is top priority. God has invited and encouraged me to enter into his presence and present my requests. I must seek him out in secret (Matthew 6:6). I must keep at it (Luke 18:1). I must come boldly to him (Hebrews 4:16).

Prayer is related to my worship (Matthew 6:9). I think that worship is the most important activity I can perform. God is worthy of all the praise and honor I can ever give to him. Almost every commandment and exhortation is fulfilled in worship as well as most of the promises. Indeed, "hallowed be thy name" (Matthew 6:9).

Praying is related to my faith (Matthew 21:22). Prayer is an expression of what I truly believe. I have to be fully surrendered to God. Worship and faith are a result of obedience and desire.

Praying is related to my helper (Romans 8:26). Likewise, the Spirit also helps my infirmities . . . he maketh intercession for me. Prayer is a cooperative ministry and I am not alone. He is only a breath away. I am overwhelmed when I think of the Holy Spirit's participation in my life. When I cannot think and even respond, he is present helping me. I can go through any difficulty when I have this assurance.

Prayer is related to my intercession (Ephesians 6:18). I will persevere for the saints because he has called me to pray. The people I come in contact with become my prayer ministry. I was not designed to live an isolated life. I am a member of one body which is reflective in the local church. My interdependence is seen in the way I am dependent upon another through prayer.

Praying is related to the will of God (I John 5:14). I have had to learn to mix the Word of God with faith. Learning to pray the will of God into actuality in my own life as well as others is an ongoing experience. My fellowship with God has grown. Prayer to God through his Son and the guidance of the Holy Spirit has brought sweet communion and intimacy with the supreme being. This is all possible through God's grace.

My effectiveness in prayer is based upon my dependence upon God. I am conscious of my need for him. Reliance is a daily thing that occupies my life. I do not start without his presence. I realize that my existence is provided by the Almighty (Acts 17:28). Self-sufficiency is dissolved through a deep reliance.

I am learning that transparency in life before God's presence is needed. He needs not only my words but my thoughts and feelings. Any doubts or questions have to be brought to him. He wants me to confide in him and I must be open. Every part of my heart has to be transparent to the Lord.

Reliance and transparency leads to unwavering faith (James 1:5-8). A strong faith will produce a willingness on God's part to grant my petitions. I cannot live with a double-mind. It is only one direction I have to follow. My divided allegiance cannot be in my life. Jesus Christ has to be Lord no matter what the cost. My life has to be characterized by a confident trust.

Unwavering faith, transparency and reliance need to be motivated by an intense fervor. I need to have determination in my prayer life. No matter what the circumstances, I have to practice wrestling with persistence. Then I have to, with confidence, leave the matter with the Lord and he will answer. Blessings from God will come when I obey God's way.

22

How Often Do We Deny Jesus Christ?

In chapter 18 of the Gospel of John, I discovered several topics to think about. Peter's words of denial, "I am not" (v17) would not leave my thoughts. At first, I thought how could he deny Jesus? He was close to the Lord. I know in my studies that the days in which Peter lived were very difficult. It would take a lot of conviction, confidence and courage to stand up.

What about today? I could not help but join Peter in his weeping and sadness when he didn't have the strength to stand up for Jesus. How many times during a day do I fall short in being a good testimony for Jesus? I confess that I could be a better witness. There are times that I could say something but I don't. There are times I am embarrassed to say anything. There are times I just make excuses that are not valid. There are times I don't feel like it. There are times I think I don't have enough knowledge to defend the truth. There are other people that can do a better job. There are times I just think that I want to be accepted and not laughed at. There are times my own sensitivity gets in the way and I think the suffering is not worth it. I think there is too much of me in the way. Of course, the way of life today is "meism." I must refocus my thinking and I can become a fearless testimony for Jesus. I must claim the power of the Holy Spirit who dwells within me to produce the strength I need.

It has always been hard for me to open up and share even though I have shared many times in witnessing. Every ministry I have been in has brought new challenges. It is not dread nor extreme fear that have followed me. It is because of my supersensitive nature. Confrontation and debate with an agreeable taste is alright but when does that ever happen? I can disagree agreeably. I really have to rely upon 2 Timothy 1:7 which says "God hath not given me the spirit of fear."

I am able to establish a daily bold witness through applying the text. To overcome personal weakness and inadequacies, I must be conscious of God's presence. If I am fearful, lack confidence or just uneasy, I must place myself into the text and share with the Holy Spirit who is my comforter. I have to claim the verse for every activity. I have to pray for the right opportunities to come to my attention. I must ask for God's courage and boldness. I must respond with love for Jesus Christ and be ready to glorify him. I must be sound in my judgment and be prepared with the strength of the Holy Spirit. When I lean on "the everlasting arm" of the Lord, the promise will be fulfilled.

I have seen it work in a variety of experiences. In music, I have created, developed and established many instrumental music education curriculums. I have prayed for the right opportunity and, through certain circumstances, they have opened up. When I started the programs at some of the schools, I was driving past the school and an inner voice (my subconscious) told me to stop and investigate the opportunity. I asked for courage from God and when I asked to talk with the administrator, he was already prepared for me. The administration and other officials had previously discussed the idea but did not know what step to take after that. I was able to establish the curriculum because God gave me a passion and love for music and children. I realized that students should have the right to glorify God in this way. I think the Lord gave me boldness to enter unknown territory because of the love he had produced in me. He also gave a sound mind and good judgment. The development of self-confidence through knowledge and previous preparations prepared the way. I did not have to enter into the opportunity with embarrassment because I was confident in what I was doing. God had promised the spirit of fearlessness. Power, strength, courage, boldness, love, passion, deep desire and a sound mind have been integrated together to bring success. It is fellowship with Jesus that makes it possible.

In ministry, this verse has paid big dividends. I was on the way to visit a family from my church because pastoral visitation was a worthwhile ministry in my church. I have always been organized and was following my agenda. This family was on the list to visit. As I traveled, I reached the top of the hill and came to a four-way stop. I had been praying for the right thing to talk about and would always leave a pastoral prescription with encouragement. My thoughts were deep in listening to the Lord. My spirit kept saying that I should turn left instead of right to the family's home. If I turned to the left, I would end up at the hospital. I didn't have anyone at the hospital to visit at this time. This would mess up my schedule, but the urge was so great that I was compelled to turn toward the hospital. I took an aggressive step and followed the inner voice.

When I reached the hospital, a nurse was waiting to direct me to a hospital room where a patient had asked for me. She was dying and was encouraged, by listening to a combined church music cantata that I had directed, to call for my presence. My visit was welcomed and spirit-led. After our visit, the Lord gave her peace and rest on her last few hours on earth. She would be soon in the very presence of her Savior. I was conscious of the Lord's presence. I was willing to follow whatever God wanted even if it didn't follow the previously prepared plan. I was in tune with his will. I walked into unknown territory without fear because the Holy Spirit was present with his power. I lost myself to the need of the hour and wondered how I could be a servant to this dear lady that needed security and a sense of God's presence. I do not remember what was said but sound judgment and spiritual enlightenment was shared. The love of God was manifested and it motivated my direction into this changed plan of action. The Lord does not give fear but confidence as we fulfill his plan and rely on Him.

Why Did Jesus Christ Die?

The trial before Pilate is given more space in this gospel than the others. As we read about the events that place, the characters and their questions become the central point of interest. I think it is a trial of Pilate before Christ instead of Christ before Pilate. "Pilates attitudes reveals that he passed from indifference through curiosity to intense concern, and then because he did not dare to act on what he knew was right, he gave way to hesitation, fear, arrogance and bitterness." The story of Pilate is the tragedy of unbelief.

The narrative is given that we may believe "that ye also may believe" (John 19:35). The scene before us includes the act of crucifixion, the placing of the title on the cross, the division of the garments, the provision for Jesus' mother, the final cry from the cross and the piercing with the spear. Jesus Christ was not a defeated martyr but a triumphant victor. "He . . . gave up his spirit" (19:30).

Recently I was visiting a 95-year-old that shared with me a note in her Bible. That note has provided the difference between unbelief and belief. It reminds her of the decision of faith she made a long time ago and wants to share with others today. It is the Romans plan for redemption. "No other portion of Holy Scripture so completely sets forth the great doctrines of the Christian faith as does the book of Romans." I always encourage new believers to read and study the gospel of John and then follow it with Romans.

Here is the simple plan of salvation found in Romans. Romans 3:23 "All have sinned, and come short of the glory of God." The 'glory of God' refers to Jesus Christ (John 1:14). This means we do not measure up to the sinlessness of Jesus Christ. 'All have sinned' emphasizes the standard. We have missed the mark. We can be justified by faith (v.28). It is through God's grace alone that provides the way.

Romans 6:23 "For the wages of sin is death, but the gift of God is eternal life through Jesus Christ our Lord." We cannot measure up to God's standards (sin). There is a wage to be paid and it is death (separation from God for eternity). Gods unmerited favor (grace) is the way to eternal life.

Romans 5:8 "God commendeth his love toward us, in that, while we were yet sinners, Christ died for us." God's divine plan provided the way (Galatians 4:1-5). At the time of our greatest need, nothing but the blood of Jesus would satisfy that need. The Lord Jesus Christ died not only for those void of morality but for those who were actively opposed to God. God demonstrated his love by sending Jesus Christ to die for us while we were yet sinners.

Romans 10:9,10 "Say with your mouth, 'Jesus is Lord.' Believe in your heart that God raised him from the dead and you will be saved. With your heart, you believe and are made right with God. With your mouth, you say that Jesus is Lord and you are saved." This is our confession of faith.

What is Supernatural About Jesus Christ's Death?

I love the words "he saw and believed" (20:8). John, the disciple who leaned on Jesus' breast at the last supper, and who regarded him as his best friend, was left desolate after the crucifixion. He ran to the tomb with perhaps a dimmer of hope that Jesus might manifest himself again. The teaching of Christ's resurrection now began to dawn on him and his sight turned to faith as he realized that Christ had risen again from the dead.

There is adequate evidence that the resurrection of Christ took place. A supernatural restoration of Jesus happened. The first bit of evidence was the fact that the door of the tomb was open. John leaves the impression in our mind that it was done by divine intervention.

Who would have moved it? There is no logical reason for anyone to have moved it except God.

A second witness was the appearance of the grave clothes. The two disciples gazed intently at the grave clothes without a body in them. Jesus had passed through the grace clothes.

The personal appearance of Jesus provides direct evidence of his resurrection. In each instance, the physical reality of Jesus was stressed. He was recognized, was heard and touched. The Christians of the first century believed in the physical return of Jesus from the dead. The key to the book is "Become not unbelieving, but believers" (v. 30,31). The solution for the problem of unbelief is to accept the resurrection as a fact. The Bible is dependable and the witnesses are numerous.

I believe the most important fact of history is Jesus Christ's resurrection. Take time to examine and weigh the evidence of those who have written about them. Determine for yourself the valued evidence of historical facts. From a legal standpoint, "there is more evidence for the historical fact of the resurrection of Jesus Christ than for just about any other event in history." The prediction of Jesus Christ's resurrection in the Gospels provide authority and confirmation of the truth. Faith is not irrational but creditable. Belief is based upon an intelligent response to the historical facts and on the basis of witnesses. The study of the resurrection has to be done without prejudice, preconceived notions or conclusions. We have to let the evidence speak for itself. Allow one of the five hundred people that saw Jesus after the resurrection share their testimony. If you do not believe me, you can ask them. If we have responded to Jesus Christ through belief, we will have the evidence within us.

What Motivates Active Faith in Jesus Christ's Death and Resurrection?

As I enter the last chapter, I have had to return to my childhood and sing "Jesus loves me, this I know, for the Bible tells me so." The love of God is the greatest thing in the universe. The Bible says, "But God, who is rich in mercy, out of the great love with which he loved us . . ." (Ephesians 2:4). The word 'love' goes far beyond my own ideas. Love found in the Bible refers to general affection, friendship, sensuality and sacrifice. It is way beyond my comprehension. The Scriptures say, "in the love of Christ which surpasses knowledge that you may be filled with all the fullness of God" (Ephesians 3:18,19). His love is infinite and cannot be exhausted. I cannot understand it but I am experiencing it.

A favorite verse in my childhood and senior years is "God so loved" (John 3:16). In his love, he gives the best of gifts. He has given himself. There is nothing that anyone can give greater than that. God gave himself in Jesus. I am assured of that kind of love. His love is also sovereign. He is free to love whom he chooses. He is not influenced by anything and his love lies only in himself. "He destined us in love to be his sons through Jesus Christ" (Ephesians 1:5,6). The final word description of love is eternal, "who shall separate us from the love of Christ?" (Romans 8:35-39).

His love is found in eternity past and eternity future and it has no end. Nothing can separate me from his love. God has decreed that it is only in Christ that his great, infinite, giving, sovereign and eternal love for sinners may be known. I am assured of his love. I am grateful for his love and for the infusion of that love in my own heart. Through Christs' sacrifice, death, resurrection, ascension and through Pentecost, I am complete. I have to accept his love and give my priority to loving him. Jesus said, "Lovest thou me?" (21:15). I have been motivated with that question. Do I love God completely? Is it with deep emotion and appreciation? Is it pure and with intensity? Is it spontaneous? Is it with affection and intimacy? If I make the decision to love with these thoughts in mind, I will be empowered by him.

Sources

Barnes, Albert — Matthew and Mark — Baker Book House 1956

Barnes, Albert — Luke and John — Baker Book House

Berry, George R — The Interlinear — Greek English New Testament, Zondervan Publishing House

Halley, Henry — Bible Handbook — Chicago, Illinois 1927

Martin, Alfred — John-Life Through Believing, Moody Press 1959

Tenney, Merrill C. — John, the Gospel of Belief, Wm Eerdman's Publishing Company 1953

Unger and Merrill F — Unger's Bible Dictionary, Moody Press 1957

Wuest, Kenneth S — The Gospels, Wm Eerdman's Publishing Company 1955

Falwell, Jerry - Liberty Bible Commentary, The Old-Time Gospel Hour 1983

Wiersbee, Warren — Be Compassionate, Chariot Victor 1988

Barclay, William — The Gospel of Luke, Westminster Press 1956

Boice, James Montgomery — Foundations of the Christian Faith, Intervarsity Press 1986

Evans, Tony — Our God is Awesome, Moody Press 1994

Geisler, Norman — Unshakable Foundations, Bethany House 2001

Matthew, Victor — Daily Affirmation of Faith, Notes 1980

Unknown, From The Heart — The Life Model 2010

Graham, Billy — Nearing Home, Thomas Nelson 2011

Stowell, Joseph M. — Eternity, Moody Press 1995

Jeremiah, David — When Your World Falls Apart, Thomas Nelson 2000

DeHaan, M.R — Hebrews, Zondervan Publishing House 1959

MacArthur, John — The MacArthur New Testament Commentary Hebrews, Moody Bible Institute 1983

McDowell, Josh & Bill Wilson — A Ready Defense, Thomas Nelson Inc. 1993

All Scripture quotations are taken from the King James Version of the Bible. Thomas Nelson Incorporated, 1976 and New International Readers Version, International Bible Society, 1998

Acknowledgements

I appreciate all the people that God has used to influence me. Many of these thoughts have come to my memory over the past seventy-five years through sermon notes, lectures, conversations, meditations and reading. I have not knowingly withheld any significant reference from others in my devotional. To the best of my knowledge, all statements and information are true and correct and given credit. Everyone I have come in contact with should be given credit. Discovering God's Love is a constant source of strength, support and security for me and I hope for you.

www.ingramcontent.com/pod-product-compliance
Lightning Source LLC
Chambersburg PA
CBHW070103080526
44586CB00013B/1171